<section>Praise for
*The Secrets Women Keep*

"Just as strychnine is poison to our bodies, so are secrets for our souls. Dr. Jill gently helps us sort through those toxic secrets that are poisoning our systems and leads us, then, to a place of understanding and renewed emotional health. This is a life-changing book. I'm willing to bet my upper porcelain veneers you will agree!"

—MARILYN MEBERG
Women of Faith® speaker and
author, *Love Me, Never Leave Me*

"Dr. Jill Hubbard is an insightful and smart therapist who understands how powerful secrets can be in a person's life. She approaches the subject with sensitivity and offers help that brings healing."

—DR. LINDA MINTLE
Author, therapist, and resident expert,
*Living the Life* television

"For those of us who learned early how to closely guard things that might be frowned upon by our families or even others, we need help to see how much power our secrets hold over us. Here's that help. Dr. Jill's insights into the unhealthiness of secrets challenge us to look at what we never had the courage to admit—she offers us hope."

—JAN STOOP, PhD
Coauthor, *Better Than Ever: Seven Secrets of Great Marriages*

# THE SECRETS WOMEN KEEP

## What Women Hide and
## the Truth that Brings Them Freedom

## DR. JILL HUBBARD

*with* RACHELLE GARDNER

THOMAS NELSON
*Since 1798*

NASHVILLE   DALLAS   MEXICO CITY   RIO DE JANEIRO   BEIJING

*The Secrets Women Keep* provides information of a general nature and is not to be used as an alternative method for conditions requiring the services of a personal physician or other health-care professional.

Information contained in this book or in any other publication, article, or Web site should not be considered a substitute for consultation with a board-certified doctor to address individual medical needs. Individual facts and circumstances will determine the treatment that is most appropriate. *The Secrets Women Keep* publisher and its author, Jill Hubbard, PhD, disclaim any liability, loss, or damage that may result in the implementation of the contents of this book.

Published in Nashville, Tennessee, by Thomas Nelson. Thomas Nelson is a registered trademark of Thomas Nelson, Inc.

Published in association with the literary agency of WordServe Literary Group, Ltd., 10152 S. Knoll Circle, Highlands Ranch, Colorado 80130.

Thomas Nelson, Inc. titles may be purchased in bulk for educational, business, fund-raising, or sales promotional use. For information, please e-mail SpecialMarkets@ThomasNelson.com.

Unless otherwise noted, Scripture quotations are taken from the Holy Bible: New International Version®. © 1973, 1978, 1984 by International Bible Society. Used by permission of Zondervan Publishing House. All rights reserved.

Scripture quotation marked MSG is from *The Message* by Eugene H. Peterson. © 1993, 1994, 1995, 1996, 2000. Used by permission of NavPress Publishing Group. All rights reserved.

Scripture quotations marked NLT are from the Holy Bible, New Living Translation, © 1996. Used by permission of Tyndale House Publishers, Inc., Wheaton, Illinois 60189. All rights reserved.

### Library of Congress Cataloging-in-Publication Data

Hubbard, Jill.
    The secrets women keep : what women hide and the truth that brings them freedom / Jill Hubbard, with Rachelle Gardner.
        p. cm.
    Includes bibliographical references.
    ISBN 978-0-7852-2816-5 (trade paper)
    1. Women—Religious aspects—Christianity. 2. Women—Psychology. 3. Christian women—Religious life. 4. Femininity—Religious aspects—Christianity. 5. Femininity. I. Gardner, Rachelle. II. Title.
    BT704.H79 2008
    248.8'43—dc22                                                                  2008022922

*Printed in the United States of America*
08 09 10 11 12 RRD 6 5 4 3 2 1

To Nancy Anne Smith, PsyD,
for dedicating her life to helping others with their secrets
and
to the women who have shared
their secrets with me.

# CONTENTS

# Foreword

When I was working on *The Secrets Men Keep*, I had a big wake-up call. I realized that even though I've spent most of my working life being as transparent and open as possible, I still had secrets. There were still battles to be won, still faults I'm trying to overcome. Some things, I still keep to myself.

I was humbled by this revelation and became even more committed to sharing with others how important—and freeing—it is to strive for a secret-free life. Most of all, I wanted to let people know that secrets are universal, and if you're keeping them, you're not alone.

Men and women share the tendency to keep things secret, but the nature of their secrets differ in many ways. That's why Dr. Jill has written this book for women. I've known her for twenty years, and I can honestly say she is the wisest female psychologist I've ever known. Dr. Jill is brilliant in her insight, kindness, and ability to see past the symptoms toward solutions, and she shows that in this book. Her Christlike, compassionate nature comes through in everything she does, and I know you'll experience that here.

I've listened and talked to women calling in to our radio program, *New Life Live!*, for more than a decade, and I've come to the conclusion that we all suffer when we keep truths about ourselves hidden—from our significant others, from the world, and most notably, from ourselves. Everyday callers experience a new freedom and hopefulness, simply through the act of sharing their secret with us on *New Life Live!*, often speaking it aloud for the very first time. It may have been the scariest thing they've ever done, but they quickly realize it was a necessary step toward a more authentic and successful life.

In fact, many of the calls we receive can be boiled down to some kind of secret, something we don't want to face or admit. Just recently we spoke to a woman whose husband was using pornography—she didn't know how to deal with it, mostly because she was concerned about keeping anyone from finding out. We spoke to another woman who has been ignoring and hiding her husband's and daughter's alcohol abuse. Another did not know how to deal with her husband's adultery. In all of these cases, the first step toward solutions and healing is to stop trying so hard to keep the problem hidden. Let it out into the light so that God and others can help.

Have you ever felt that you are living a life that is not quite authentic? That people don't know who you really are? When you live with secrets, you're not able to be fully known by others. But a life without secrets is a life of freedom, where you can be your real self, where you are the same on the outside as you are on the inside. Dr. Jill has written a book that shows you how to get to that place and find an emotionally healthy way to live.

By talking about your secrets—to yourself, to God, and to others—you will find healing. Take comfort in one thing above all: you are not alone. Everyone struggles with keeping things hidden. But God knows your secrets already, and He is waiting for you to open up to Him. There are others who will be open to hearing your truth, too, whether spouses, siblings, friends, pastors, or counselors.

Take this journey with Dr. Jill, and find a new level of joy and peace by being honest, authentic, and free of the burden of secrets.

—STEPHEN ARTERBURN

# A Note from Dr. Jill

This book contains dozens of accounts of real women and their secrets. To each of them I am grateful. Their willingness to take a risk to reveal their hearts, their stories, and their pain—and to trust me with them—is something I do not take lightly. So a heartfelt *thank you* to all of you, known and unknown, who contributed to this work.

In saying that, I want to make it clear that all identities have been protected, and though you may recognize yourself or someone you know in these pages, be assured it's only because we are all more similar than we think. Nothing in this book can reveal the identity of any specific person.

You'll note that some of the stories are in third person and include the woman's name. Again, all names and identifying details have been changed, and most of the third-person examples are composites of a number of women, based on my years of clinical practice as a psychologist and my involvement with New Life Ministries and the *New Life Live!* radio program. Their stories are real, but they do not represent any particular person. If any of the details here happen to match up to those of someone you know, it is coincidental.

The second type of story you'll find in this book is the first-person account (the snippets where women recount their secrets in their own voices, using *I* and *me*). These stories are from women who wrote to the *New Life Live!* Secrets Blog in response to my requests on the radio for women to share their secrets. There are no names on these stories; in fact, women were instructed *not* to include their names or e-mail addresses, and our Web site didn't track the addresses of the letters sent to us. So the stories are completely anonymous. In many cases, I've included the women's words verbatim as they were originally written; others have been lightly edited for grammar and punctuation or to camouflage identifying details, but in no way was the content or meaning changed.

If you are a secret-bearer, I am offering up prayers for you, asking God to use these words to comfort your heart and lead you to a life of freedom in Christ, a life that is not hidden. I am keeping in mind Philippians 1:3–6, and I offer it to you now: "I thank my God every time I remember you. In all my prayers for all of you, I always pray with joy because of your partnership in the gospel from the first day until now, being confident of this, that he who began a good work in you will carry it on to completion until the day of Christ Jesus." Please remember the importance of this fact: God began a good work in you, and He *will* complete it.

As you read this book, I pray you find hope and healing in knowing that you are not alone. The God of the universe knows your secrets, and He loves you deeply, regardless of what they are. He is opening his arms to you, ready to take on your burdens. Walk with me now, out of the dark and into the light of His love.

—Dr. Jill

# Part One

# THE TRUTH ABOUT SECRETS

## Chapter 1

# Everyone Has Secrets

I filed for bankruptcy last year. I am so ashamed of the mess I have made of my finances. I have not told anyone about the bankruptcy, not even my family.

✦ ✦ ✦

My secret is that although I seem completely together spiritually and I know a lot about the Bible, I'm always afraid that I'm not really saved. I worry that I'm not the real deal, and I'm afraid that I will go to hell.

✦ ✦ ✦

My husband doesn't have a strong libido. The secret is, we don't have sex anymore. For a while it was just infrequent, and now it's been a few months since we were intimate. Who on earth could relate to this? Most women have the opposite problem, so there's no one I can talk to.

Everyone has secrets. I do, and you do. Whether they're small and harmless or huge and explosive, we all carry around little pieces of ourselves that we choose not to share with anyone else.

What's your secret? Take a moment and admit it to yourself. Is it difficult to face?

Every week, I talk to people on the radio program *New Life Live!* with Stephen Arterburn. We speak with people from all over the country, advising them about what concerns them most in their spiritual, emotional, and relational lives. When I began talking about women's secrets, the reaction was immense, immediate, and heartfelt. Women called in to the program and wrote in to our Secrets Blog, revealing their stories. For some, all they needed was permission to unburden themselves in a secure environment, knowing that someone would care about what they had to say, and *whoosh!* . . . the responses flooded in. Women poured out their hearts, expressing emotions they'd never shared, spilling truths that had never seen the light of day. Many said this was the first time they'd ever spoken about their secret. It was safe. It was anonymous. It was a first step out of the darkness of their hidden life.

We also conducted a national survey of more than one thousand women (in addition to the responses we received on the Secrets Blog) in which we asked about their secrets. This book reflects those results too.

If you've picked up this book, something about the idea of secrets probably resonates with you. Maybe you want to know why you keep them or why they weigh on you. Perhaps you want to know what's wrong with keeping secrets or if there are times when secrets are necessary. Maybe you're interested to find out what kinds of secrets other women are keeping. You want to know that you are okay and that you are not alone.

If there's anything my research for this book has shown me, it's just that—you are *definitely* not alone.

You may have opened this book thinking it was about the secrets women keep from men. Or you might even be a man trying to sneak a peek at what really goes on inside the head of a woman. But that's not really what this book is about. It is more than the secrets women keep from men; it's about the secrets we keep from anyone or everyone, even from ourselves. It's those pieces of truth that weigh on us because we're carrying them alone. We're going to look at all the major things women keep secrets about and explore why we feel we can't share these parts of ourselves with anyone else.

We will spend most of this book exploring the secrets that are harmful to our lives, our relationships, and our mental and emotional health. But obviously, not all secrets are "bad." There are certain things about ourselves that other people don't need to know. There are secrets shared between husbands and wives that don't belong in the outside world. There are business secrets we're obligated to keep because of competition. There are fun secrets that we hold on to until just the right moment to turn them into wonderful surprises. Sometimes we are asked to keep others' secrets and confidences and realize they are not ours to share. Even God has secrets, things He chooses not to reveal to us, as indicated in Deuteronomy 29:29: "The secret things belong to the LORD."

The Bible even instructs us to keep some things secret from others—our private prayers and how much we give to church and charities, for instance. We are not to parade them for all the world to see (Matt. 6:5–8, 16–18). Those are secrets God wants us to share with Him alone.

Some secrets are "good" in that, when shared, they can become the basis for close relationships. The person with whom you share your secret can be a best friend, sibling, parent, or spouse. The fact that you share the deepest parts of yourself with that person means you trust him or her, at least to a certain degree. We use secrets to deepen relationships, to tell someone, "You matter to me." Conversely, keeping secrets from someone we love usually harms the relationship.

## Why Do We Keep Secrets?

Think about the secrets you're keeping—whether from your spouse, your friends, or from the world. What makes you keep those tidbits to yourself? Would you be embarrassed or mortified if people knew this about you? Would you feel vulnerable and exposed? Do you live in fear that someone might find out?

Secrets are a way we hide our true selves from the world. Shame and fear keep us from letting others know who we really are, what mistakes we've made, and the ways we feel we don't measure up.

> My secret is that I am not "enough" and never will be.
> That I am not fulfilling my purpose for God, that I am no
> longer attractive and sexy enough for my husband to want
> me, that I am not productive enough at my job, that I am
> not available enough nor have the energy to be there, physi-
> cally, emotionally, and spiritually for my adult children.

Christian women especially seem to feel the need to hide the ways they're not perfect. We make bad choices like everyone else; we sin and sometimes turn our backs on God, but the idea of letting others know about the ways we fail strikes fear into our hearts. Tammy Maltby, in her book *Confessions of a Good Christian Girl*, wrote, "Why the cover-up? We tell ourselves we must 'keep a good witness'—you know, keep God looking good. More often, I think, we do it to keep ourselves comfortable."[1]

Isn't that the truth! It's supremely *uncomfortable* for us to have our weaknesses, failings, or disappointments on parade for others to see.

Many of us keep secrets out of guilt over sin or failing. Unfortunately, the more we live in our guilt all alone, the easier it is for the enemy to use our guilt to keep us feeling shameful, unworthy, *not good enough*. We feel more and more like we're living in the dark, lonely and worthless. As long as we stay in the dark with our secrets, we allow the enemy to keep us feeling that way. Bringing our secrets out of the dark and into the light can allow us to gain perspective on them, see that we're not alone, and understand that regardless of how "bad" the secret is, it doesn't have to define us. We are still loved and lovable.

We women have a keen sense of needing to live up to expectations—those from our families, our culture, our Christian community, and those we place on ourselves. We tend to have unrealistic expectations about what we *should* be able to accomplish and about what life was going to be like. But life usually doesn't follow our expectations. Our experience of reality doesn't match with what we've been led to believe our reality should be.

So we hide our reality.

It's one thing for us to realize we're not "measuring up." It's quite another for our spouses, families, and friends to realize it and reflect it back to us. That's just not okay, is it? So we keep our secrets.

Most of us learned to keep secrets when we were very young. We figured out by the age of three or four that it's possible to keep information from someone. We'd say in a singsong voice, "I've got a secret"—and it was often something wonderful, or at least something harmless. As we grew older, we learned we could keep secrets as a way of protecting ourselves, usually from the discipline of our parents and teachers. Eventually we discovered we could keep secrets as a way of having power over others. Knowledge is power, and the more we kept to ourselves, the more powerful we felt.

Some of us grew up in families where secret keeping was the norm, even required for the family to function. Everything from abuse to addiction to all kinds of destructive behaviors was purposely ignored, the proverbial "elephant in the room." My friend Denise experienced years of confusion from this type of family secret keeping.

My parents divorced when I was four, and two years later when my mother remarried, my father gave up his parental rights and disappeared, leaving me to be raised by my mother and stepfather. From then on, nobody in the family

ever mentioned—not even once—my real dad. Nobody
talked about him. Nobody referred to him in any way.
Nobody acknowledged that I'd spent the first six years of
my life completely attached to my dad, adoring him in
that unique way that daughters love their fathers. He was
simply gone, and the people around me conspired to pretend that he'd actually never existed.

This might seem like an extreme example, but a surprising number of families keep the peace by hiding or ignoring huge pieces of
their reality. Keeping the secret serves everyone. Well, at least all the
adults. The desire for some people to create the picture of the life
they want by erasing the mistakes can be very strong. We tend to
cover up messiness so we can present our lives as neat and tidy.

Many adults also live under the myth that it is better not to
bring up an uncomfortable subject with children so as not to upset
them. (As if not talking about something could control a person's
internal thoughts.) While we do need to protect children and avoid
dumping adult burdens on them, not acknowledging the obvious is
craziness. And when we lie, pretend, and alter reality, we actually do
more damage to children's ability to process life, causing them to
doubt their own perceptions, to distrust what they hear, see, and
think. Children are not resilient, as the cliché goes; they are actually
absorbent and take in everything around them.

No wonder secret keeping comes so naturally to us when many
of us grew up in a culture of secrets. We learn through everyday
example that it's not okay to be human or fallible. We learn it's necessary to hide who we are. This becomes normal for us. As Gail Saltz
said in her book, *Anatomy of a Secret Life*, "Even a secret life as extreme
as Tony Soprano's is normalized through the collusion of the other
members of his household, who all depend on his being a mobster
to satisfy their . . . desires for money and status."[2]

Secrets—as much as they *seem* to serve a worthy purpose—can
lead to the total destruction of a relationship, a family, a job, or a life.

*Chapter 2*

---

# What's Wrong with Keeping Secrets?

I believe the secrets we're keeping are slowly but surely destroying us. That's a pretty dramatic statement, I know. But think about it. A secret eats away at you, and as time passes, it seems to grow and fester. It becomes more and more of a burden.

A secret is a part of ourselves we're keeping hidden in darkness, but it cries out for the light. We know instinctively that we can't flourish in the dark, so as long as we are hiding pieces of our truth from the light, we experience a disturbance in our hearts and souls. It might be subtle, like an undercurrent of feeling that something's not right. Or it might be overwhelming, determining the shape of our relationships and our lives.

When we are going through life acting as one person on the outside, while we're really a different person on the inside, we can't have peace. We know something's off. There's an acute sense of dissonance when our interiors and exteriors don't match. It's as if we are an orchestra, and the brass is playing a Mozart concerto while the strings are playing a Beethoven sonata. It sounds awful! We cringe at the dreadful sounds—and when we have secrets, our hearts and souls cringe at the terrible noise within us.

It requires an enormous reservoir of energy to maintain two distinct selves—the external front we show the world, and the internal, *true* self. This pretense drains us and robs us of the energy we could be using in countless other ways, from improving our relationships to deepening our spiritual lives to putting the laundry away and making dinner. Getting our insides and outsides to more closely match is an important goal in psychotherapy. The more aligned we are, internally and externally, the more real we can be. "What you see is what you get" is a trusted motto. We simply can't live full, passionate lives of integrity if we are not being authentic. Having secrets is a sure way to avoid authenticity.

The truth is, as much as we might feel safe in hiding our secrets, we know we can't hide from God. So we are really just fooling ourselves. "'Can anyone hide in secret places so that I cannot see him?' declares the LORD. 'Do not I fill heaven and earth?'" (Jer. 23:24).

Realizing we can't hide from God makes us feel a bit foolish when we're using all our resources to stay hidden. But still, we rationalize that even though God can see us, it's okay to keep things hidden from other people.

The Bible repeatedly calls us out of the darkness and into the light. Jesus warns that it's futile to try to keep things hidden. He said, "There is nothing concealed that will not be disclosed, or hidden that will not be made known" (Matt. 10:26).

When we keep secrets about ourselves, it's like we're constantly saying, "I'm not good enough. The truth about me is *not okay*." And when we have something to hide, it affects how we approach every aspect of life. It holds us back from engaging in true intimacy. It keeps us from living fully and expressing ourselves honestly. And it makes us unable to fully accept the love, grace, and forgiveness that God is eager to give.

We kid ourselves that as long as we keep our secrets to ourselves, we'll be fine. The problem is that we spend our lives running just ahead of our secrets—constantly maneuvering to keep from being discovered. But eventually our secrets catch up with us. We can't keep from thinking about them; we can't stay detached from them. And soon, instead of being in control of our secrets, they are in control of us.

## DIFFERENT KINDS OF SECRETS

There are probably as many different secrets as there are women. They generally fall into two categories: those that involve sinful or immoral behavior, and those that don't. It's an important distinction that will affect how you deal with your secret. It will affect who you might want to talk with and how to begin healing. It will determine whether there is a specific behavior that needs to change in order for healing to come about.

Some women are keeping secrets that involve sinful activity— theirs or someone else's. Maybe they had an affair or had an abortion. Maybe their husband is addicted to pornography. Maybe they are a late-night binger on food, shopping networks, or alcohol. Maybe somebody they trusted abused them or is still abusing them. If your secret is that you are addicted to a fantasy world involving romance novels, soap operas, Internet flirtations, or pornography, the crucial issue is stopping the behavior. You have to seek help and answers relative to the depth of involvement to change the behavior in order to get rid of the secrecy and begin working on the underlying secret—your pain.

Many more women are keeping secrets *not* about sinful behavior but about their sense of failure, their disappointment with life, or their daily struggles to measure up. They are trying to find fulfillment but instead find dashed expectations and disillusionment at every turn. They're not engaging in a specific sinful behavior, yet they're not engaging fully in life either. They are angry, discontented, or sad. And they don't tell anybody.

So our secrets may differ in whether they involve sinful behavior, but psychologically, they're all the same in that they keep us feeling that our true selves are not worthy, not good enough. They keep us feeling shameful.

One of the purposes of this book is to let you know that you are not alone in the keeping of secrets. In these pages, you're going to read many honest (and often heartbreaking) accounts from women who've been willing to share with us. We have heard from more than two thousand women about the secret issues that plague them, and more than nine hundred of these took the time to write out the vivid details. I'm including some of these accounts throughout the book, to illustrate the widespread prevalence of women's secrets and to help you understand that healing comes from bringing our hidden selves into the light.

As women we tend to assume that we're alone in our problems. We often think that nobody else feels this or feels that as strongly and deeply as we do while all along thousands of others are suffering alone, thinking nobody else could possibly understand. One of the quotes at the start of chapter 1 is from a woman whose husband isn't interested in intimate relations, and she wrote, "Most women have the opposite problem, so there's no one I can talk to." Little did she know that dozens of other women wrote to me with the very same problem.

We don't know what's going on with other women. We only know what they allow us to see—what they present as their public persona. So what we end up doing is comparing our *insides* to other women's *outsides*. We believe that other women's external appearance represents all of who they really are—when that's not the case. Our exterior, public selves are only part of who we are. Women often have an active and rich internal world with commentary running rapid. The critical committee, the doubting dialogue, and our shameful or sinful secrets all keep us fearing we'll be the only one who doesn't have it all together; therefore, our secrets stay just that.

It's a vicious cycle. We keep our failures and weaknesses to our-selves so others don't see the real us. They, in turn, don't feel they can reveal their own secrets because it appears that everyone around them is basically perfect. We are all busy perfecting our facades, suffering alone, assuming we're the *only ones* with this particular problem. And all the while we're surrounded by others suffering alone in their own pain.

## What Should We Do with Our Secrets?

We know that bringing ourselves out of the dark and into the light is what can allow healing to begin. This is what stops our secrets from being burdensome. But what light is appropriate for your secret? In other words, exactly who do we begin to share our secrets with, and how do we go about moving from darkness to light?

We're certainly not talking about confessing every secret to the world. Who you bring into your confidence depends on the nature of what you're holding inside. As we go through the chapters of this book, each one addressing a specific type of secret, we'll talk about appropriate ways to bring that particular issue into the light: who to talk to, how, and why.

There are three ways in which we can safely begin moving into the light, regardless of the type of issue we're hiding.

*Be honest with ourselves about it.* Earlier I asked you to take a moment and think about your secret. Sometimes this can be much easier said than done! Especially when we have some secrets for the purpose of hiding other secrets. But the first step on the road to healing is to acknowledge our secrets, even multilayered secrets, to ourselves. After all, it's impossible to go any further—to share ourselves with anyone else—without this first step. Many of the women who wrote in to our *New Life Live!* Secrets Blog admitted this was the first time they'd shared their secrets, even the first time they'd acknowledged them to themselves. What an important milestone.

*Be honest with God about it.* Perhaps the single most freeing step you can take is to completely lay your secret on the table to God. It may be a confession, or it may be more like a pouring out of your pain and sorrow. Whatever it is, if we start by allowing God's light into our dark places, we can immediately experience some of the burden lifting. When we acknowledge that we're not alone but allowing God to help us, He's faithful to do just that.

*Be honest with a trusted counselor.* You may or may not be ready to seek counseling from a professional. Be assured that this is one of the ways we can safely acknowledge the hidden parts of ourselves and determine who else needs to be allowed inside. If you're feeling especially burdened by your secret—if it's ruling your life in some way—then I encourage you to consider seeking a safe, professional counseling environment in which to explore it.

After these first three steps, you'll be ready to decide if there's anyone else who needs to know your secret. Sometimes there is somebody close to you who deserves to know this truth about you. In other cases, you may have a close friendship that hasn't grown because of your inability to be vulnerable and transparent, and you decide to take this person into your confidence. Perhaps you need to be real with your husband, or maybe you have long-standing issues with your mother or father that could begin healing through your honesty. It's up to you to decide whether to share with a friend or family member, or with the world. But it starts with being honest with yourself, with God, and (if you choose) a professional psychotherapist.

The goal is not to air our dirty laundry for the world to see, but to stop allowing our secrets to define us. We want to put an end to secrets that hinder us in our relationships and our emotional health. Keeping our truth hidden usually means we're not pursuing solutions to our problems, which allows our troubles to grow and get worse.

It's not that we don't keep anything private. The point is that we don't need to carry around our secrets like weights. We can have the knowledge of a particular truth about ourselves, but not the weight of it. When we share the burden, even if we're sharing only with Jesus, the burden becomes much easier to bear.

Each chapter of this book looks at a different category of secrets women keep, and we'll explore them from a variety of angles. Each chapter includes these sections:

- **"Unlocking the Secret"**—we look at the secret and the different ways you may experience it.
- **"Keeping the Secret"**—we examine why you keep the secret and why it weighs on you.
- **"Think About It"**—I briefly offer some tips from a psychological perspective on how to deal with your secret.
- **"Spiritual Secrets"**—we look at biblical help for your secret.
- **"From Secrets to Solutions"**—we discuss how to strip the secret of its power by being honest with yourself, honest with God, and honest with a counselor.
- **"Praying Scripture for Your Secret"**—I offer a brief prayer based on a specific Bible verse.
- **"Recommended Resources"**—I give you a list of books and Web sites for further exploration.

As you move through this book, hearing what other women have to say and thinking more deeply about your own secrets, be aware that this can at times be a painful or scary process. It's not always fun to examine ourselves and face who we really are. But the reward is completely worth it.

Imagine living free of secrets, feeling comfortable in your own skin, never feeling as if you have to hide yourself from anyone. Imagine being able to fully experience the love and grace of Christ, to completely accept His forgiveness, to be totally open to the life He has to offer you.

Walk with me on this road of self-discovery. I promise you, it will be worth it.

*Chapter 3*

# Keeping Secrets from Ourselves

"My husband is *such* a loser."

Connie had come to me for counseling and spent the last several sessions regaling me with tales of her husband's total irresponsibility and lack of contribution to the family. She is the sole breadwinner and works full time in a demanding job. Over time, things have disintegrated to the point where she also takes almost all of the responsibility for the children, the home, the bills, and family activities. They live in an affluent area and present a picture-perfect image to the world, a family with "all the right stuff." Yet Connie's husband doesn't work and seems incapable of helping out. She's not sure how or when this happened, but she truly doesn't know how her husband spends his time and is pretty sure he's well acquainted with television, computer games, and all the latest techno-gadgets. Lately, things have gotten worse. Her husband has been spending money uncontrollably. He runs up the credit card, and Connie repeatedly bails him out financially.

Connie spends copious amounts of energy keeping the world

from finding out her secret: that she has an irresponsible husband and is completely exhausted from holding all the balls in the air. But she's missing a crucial part of the picture: *the secret she's keeping from herself.* She's not facing the reality of her own controlling nature. She doesn't require her husband to change because it would threaten her own sense of control. That's her *real* secret.

I suggested early in our therapy that Connie begin to talk to her husband, in a loving and nonaccusing way, about taking more responsibility in the home.

"I don't know," she said hesitantly. "I'd feel guilty doing that. I know it doesn't make sense . . ." Her voice trailed off as she pondered what she was saying. We explored her feelings, and she realized that to ask her husband for help would be "breaking the rules." Over the years, she and her husband had developed an unspoken system in which she does everything, he does nothing, and she bails him out of financial trouble whenever necessary. She has been hiding from herself the simple truth that she has *allowed* this system to operate in her marriage. She's been evading the reality that she shouldn't *have* to do everything, that this is an unreasonable arrangement. The avoidance permits her to continue enabling her husband's irresponsibility, keeping her in control. The couple's tacit agreement ensures that Connie is always head of the household.

For Connie, the big issue was not her husband but herself, and it was painful for her to face her own culpability for the situation in her marriage. As Connie became more willing to give up some control, she was more successful at talking with her husband lovingly, asking for what she needed from him, and refusing to fix the problems he caused himself. She no longer felt she had a secret from the world about her husband, and she was no longer able to keep secrets from herself about her need for control. This in turn enabled her to begin dealing with the real issue of why she has such a high need for control in the first place.

What Connie had to learn, and what we all need to realize, is that the secrets we're keeping from others are often a *cover* for the deeper secrets, the ones we're keeping from ourselves. And moving to a place of healing often involves facing not just our surface secrets but our deeper ones as well.

## KNOW THYSELF

One of the key underlying premises of modern psychology, as originally defined by Freud in the early 1900s, was the idea of "making the unconscious conscious." While the field of psychology has come a long way in a hundred years, we know that many of the truths it proclaims were originated by God long before. The Psalmist wrote, "Save me, O LORD, from lying lips and from deceitful tongues" (Ps. 120:2). We try to heal our hurts and emerge into healthier living by bringing into awareness the things about ourselves we've been unaware of. We try to become more authentic by uncovering and facing the truth about ourselves.

But that's difficult, isn't it? One of the reasons we keep secrets from others is that it distracts our focus from the real issues, the things we're keeping from ourselves.

How do we do this? Let's say you have an eating disorder that you are hiding from the world. You binge and purge, and the act of keeping this a secret takes a great deal of emotional energy. You think about it all the time and put tremendous effort into keeping this part of yourself hidden. But why do you have the eating disorder in the first place? Most likely as a response to something else—abuse or betrayal or a desperate feeling of unworthiness—that is simply too painful to face. The eating disorder masks the true secret within you, the one you really can't bear to look at.

Joyce is a successful executive, a wife of fourteen years, and a mother. She thinks of herself as a person with strong morals and a commitment to doing what's right. Yet she has found herself powerfully drawn to an extramarital affair that has continued off and on for several years. At times it has been a physical affair, but more often it has been an emotional relationship characterized by numerous daily contacts through e-mail, text messages, and phone calls. She has attempted several times to break off this relationship out of guilt but repeatedly just can't do it. It surprises her—in every other area of her life she is completely successful and able to accomplish her goals.

The secret consumes Joyce; she can't tell anyone except her therapist, and much of her time and energy are spent preserving this secret. If people were to find out, it would destroy the image she's so carefully crafted over the years. If her husband were to find out, she might lose her marriage and family.

Joyce's breakthrough and ability to end the affair didn't come until she finally faced the deeper secret she'd been desperately shielding herself from—for her entire life. She had been abandoned by her father at age two, then mistreated by her stepfather for more than a decade. She never experienced the real unconditional love of a father, and she has spent her adult life trying to find it. The affair has served the purpose of making her feel special, valued, and fully loved. *That's* the secret at the bottom of her double life, and facing that truth is what started her on the road to true healing. It will be a long and difficult process of therapy, rebuilding her marriage, and dealing with her childhood wounds. But Joyce has been able to gain a new perspective about her own behavior and see things more accurately, finding the strength to begin turning her life around. She wasn't able to deal with the secret she was keeping from the world until she faced the one she was hiding from herself.

The Bible confirms the importance of understanding ourselves and further reveals that it can be impossible without God's help. "Search me, O God, and know my heart," wrote David in Psalm 139:23. "Test me and know my anxious thoughts." As we talked about in chapter 1, being honest with God about who we are can be the most important step we take in finding help with our secrets; asking His help in understanding ourselves is just as important.

Jesus said, "If you hold to my teaching, you are really my disciples. Then you will know the truth, and the truth will set you free"

(John 8:31–32). To know Jesus is to know the truth, and our freedom comes from knowing Him. The idea that truth is freeing is
crucial to our understanding of ourselves. We cannot be truly free to
enjoy the blessings of this life—fulfilling relationships, a vibrant
spiritual life, and the joy of serving others—if our hearts and minds
are occupied with living a lie.

In his book, *Changes that Heal*, Henry Cloud explains that in
order to heal and grow, we need to experience not only truth but also
grace. In fact, truth without grace is deadly, just as grace with no
truth is a lie. Another way to think of grace is unconditional love—
that is, love that we don't earn or deserve; we simply receive. We
need to face the truth about ourselves, but if we don't give ourselves
grace, too, the truth can destroy us rather than set us free. Cloud
further emphasizes that both truth and grace must be grounded
and rooted in the love of redemptive time. That is, when our truths,
our secrets, come out of hiding into real time, with real people who
tell us the truth in love, then healing has a chance to take place.[1]
Please remember, as you read this book and as you uncover difficult
or painful secrets you have been keeping from yourself, to give
yourself grace as you move through your thoughts and feelings.
Accept the truth God is helping you see, and also accept His grace
and love and time frame as you face dealing with them in the reality
of His love.

Jesus said, "Come to me, all you who are weary and burdened,
and I will give you rest. Take my yoke upon you and learn from me,
for I am gentle and humble in heart, and you will find rest for your
souls. . . . For my yoke is easy and my burden is light" (Matt.
11:28–30). Jesus wants you to share your burdens with Him, and
He promises to treat you gently and allow you to find rest from your
troubles. He knows your truth, and He wants to give you grace. If
you are on a journey of discovering your own secrets, know that
Jesus wants to go with you. He is the ultimate confidant. You can
tell Him your secrets, hand Him your burdens, and rest in His
love.

# BUT I DON'T WANT TO KNOW!

There are many things we just don't *want* to know about ourselves. We try to keep these things slightly out of our awareness so we don't have to face them. It takes considerable emotional energy to keep pushing down the truth, and it's draining. Some of the things people try to avoid are truly horrible, such as abuse as a child. It's natural to want to avoid thinking about things like that. More commonly, we are trying to avoid seeing the dark side of ourselves. We prefer to see ourselves in a good light, and our minds can't wrap around the idea that we might be a good person with some bad traits. We feel that if we recognize a negative trait, it must mean we're really not the good person we thought we were. We can't integrate the good and bad in us.

So in order to avoid thinking of ourselves as bad, we keep secrets about our less-than-exemplary moments. We don't face the reality that maybe our motives aren't always good. Rather than examining ourselves and our motives, when we recognize a bad thought or intent, we don't *own it* but simply chalk it up to a bad behavior moment that really isn't characteristic of us.

If we can get to a place in which we own both the negative and positive sides of ourselves—including the unfair treatment we've received at others' hands—we will not have to be so bound up in keeping secrets from ourselves. People who are codependent—that is, enabling other people's bad behavior (similar to Connie at the beginning of this chapter)—survive by thinking of themselves as the good ones and convince themselves that the problems are not their own fault but simply the fault of the bad people around them.

In the next section, we're going to meet women who are unhappy in their marriages and unfulfilled in other relationships in their lives. They're keeping secrets about husbands, sex, friendships, affairs, and the difficulties of being single. These secrets are burdensome and, in some cases, debilitating. The unspoken deeper secrets are the ones the women may not have faced yet, the ones they haven't admitted.

For example, one of my friends has struggled for years with feeling unfulfilled in her marriage. She constantly thinks, *Why can't I be closer to my husband? Why don't we share things? Why don't I feel intimate with him?* Yet the secret she's been keeping from herself is that she chose her husband, and when she did, she had some level of awareness of his ability to be intimate. She most likely chose him because his level of comfort with closeness matched hers. She thinks she wants a closer relationship, but if she got it, could she handle it? Probably not. It's common for women to avoid admitting to themselves that their own ability and capacity for intimacy may also be limited.

Marissa is single, in her late twenties, and pursuing an advanced degree at a prestigious university. She works full time in addition to her studies and has no social life outside of work and school. She says she wants close friendships and that the secret she keeps from the world is her deep loneliness from lack of close relationships. She tends to pursue people with the idea of becoming friends, and in fact, she can pursue so intensely that she usually drives them away. In therapy, we've uncovered the real truth that if anyone pursues *her*, she devalues that person and runs the other way. Her secret is that she questions her own value and must be the one in control, the one doing the pursuing. Therefore, she's not really interested in people—she's interested in the chase and conquest that might validate her value momentarily before it slips through her fingers. She has finally seen this. Seeing it is the first step to being able to change it. Once Marissa begins learning to value herself and others for who they are and create genuine friendships, she'll no longer be harboring either the secret she kept from the world or the one she kept from herself.

Sometimes secrets are related to our false beliefs. For those who have trouble with needing to be in control, they probably have a belief that being in control means they can keep bad things from happening. Obviously this isn't true or even rational; we all know that things go wrong even in the best of circumstances. But controlling people operate under the false assumption that they can keep tragedy at bay, that they can determine outcomes in all circumstances. The secret they avoid telling themselves is that this isn't true.

We may have false beliefs about our own worthiness. If we are keeping secrets about having been abused, neglected, or abandoned either physically or emotionally as a child, it may be because of a false belief that somehow, we really *deserved* the abuse. That's quite a painful prospect; better to keep it a secret from ourselves and simply keep the whole idea of abuse far from our consciousness.

## So What Does All This Mean?

I put this chapter in the beginning because I want you to be thinking about it as you read the other chapters and consider all the different types of secrets we keep from the world. Underneath each one may be lurking another, deeper secret—usually something we don't want to face about ourselves.

As you read and process the secrets that resonate with you, don't forget to dig deeper. Ask yourself, Underneath this secret, is there another that I'm trying not to acknowledge? Ask God to search your heart and reveal truth to you. Remember, you *will* know the truth, and the truth will set you free.

*Part Two*

# SECRETS ABOUT MARRIAGE AND RELATIONSHIPS

# Chapter 4

# I'm Unhappy in My Marriage

I didn't love my husband when I agreed to marry him. I was twenty and thought I would never meet anyone else. He was nice, hardworking, and a Christian. I liked him well enough. After ten years of marriage, I feel so trapped. We have one son. We never built a firm foundation of love, so there is not much to draw from. I am at a loss, but I don't want my little boy to lose a family, so I keep quiet and pretend nothing is wrong.

As a psychologist, I spend quite a lot of time talking with people who are unhappy or having difficulties in some part of their lives, and that often means problems with marriage. I've seen and heard just about every marriage-related issue under the sun, and I've experienced some doozies myself.

Still, when I received the results of our national survey and began reading the stories of the women who wrote in to the Secrets Blog, I couldn't help but be moved. The letters reflected how desperately unhappy many women are in marriage—and that they are suffering silently.

It's *not* a secret that marriage can be hard, as anyone who's been married for more than a few years knows. The divorce rate reflects how challenging marriage is, and the widespread lack of willingness to get married at all (opting to live together or completely avoid intimate relationships) just confirms it. But what's *not* reflected in divorce statistics or the busy offices of marriage counselors is the misery people are experiencing in marriage without ever speaking of it or doing anything about it. The invisible casualties are those who are *not* filing for divorce or going for therapy, those whose marriages would be considered *long-term* and *intact* by the outside world—yet who endure silent pain and anguish.

Many women who wrote me felt trapped in their marriages, and some chalked it up to being a Christian and/or not wanting the failure of divorce.

> I feel trapped. My husband is a good Christian man, a wonderful father and grandfather. We have been married for thirty-two years, and sex was a big part of our relationship before we married. Then after we got married we had sex less and less. There were many nights I would cry myself to sleep because he had rejected my advances. Our sex life continued to dwindle, from once or twice a week, to once or twice a month, to once or twice a year, to nothing. We have argued, discussed, and talked about this problem for years. I love my husband, always have and always will. But there are times when I would like to have a different life. How do you leave someone you love just because you are not sexually fulfilled?

✦ ✦ ✦

> I don't love my husband. I don't think I ever have. Now every day is like prison. I feel trapped, scared, despondent. I have

no romantic interest in him, and I cannot be physically intimate with him. Every day is stressful and frustrating. I constantly dwell on the regret of marrying the wrong man and not listening to my instincts. I feel like a second divorce would be the ultimate failure and am therefore stuck in this contrived shell of a relationship, trying to make the best of a bad situation. At this point, I am barely hanging on and hoping for a miracle.

Women are dying inside because they don't feel loved and they don't feel any true connection in their marriage. There is a sense of hopelessness in their writing, a kind of resignation to the idea that "this is the way it is, and I can't do anything about it."

I don't think I ever really loved my husband. I love him the way I would love any member of my family, but not the way I should love my mate. Whenever I think about our future together, it seems so hopeless and dreary because I can't love him. I long to love someone completely and be the helpmate in the marriage, instead of the one who leads and figures everything out.

✦ ✦ ✦

Our marriage is miserable, and my husband is not interested in having any kind of relationship with me. He abandoned me emotionally, physically, and financially after adopting our son. We have not had any physical involvement for thirteen years. I have friends and have made a life on my own. I have lived enough years without love that I will do that, rather than put my son through the trauma of divorce.

Some women have endured being abused by their husbands but didn't say whether they've sought help from a counselor or a pastor.

The abuse is so shameful, there's a good chance they've never told anyone.

> Although my husband insists he has made the adequate changes, he continues to be verbally and emotionally abusive. He zaps my energy, and I just want to give up on the marriage.

❖ ❖ ❖

> I don't know about other women, but I have been abused by my husband for over fifteen years and I have covered it up and kept it a secret.

A surprising number of women have been suffering silently for so long that they are consumed with anger and even hatred for their husbands. Some are carrying the devastating secret that they can't wait for their husband to die.

> I hate my husband. I hate him. I try to convince myself he isn't so bad and try to focus on anything positive, but I can't seem to do that for long. I hate that he is a whiner and a liar. I hate the way he ignores our children. I hate that he seems to live to make sure I don't get to decide anything, from the plants in the yard to what I do to make a living. I'm afraid of God now because I have so much anger and hate—it is like being sucked into the dark side.

❖ ❖ ❖

> I sometimes think about if my husband died and I was financially provided for. I think about it in a fantasy way—like my life would be easier.

+ + +

I am waiting for my spouse to die. He has cheated on me throughout the marriage and has exposed me to various diseases. I have not left him because of our kids—they want him here. How awful, right? This is my really ugly secret.

These examples are extreme. If we look at the general population of all married people, many will say they're not always happy in marriage, but only a small percentage report this level of misery. Yet that's the very reason I've included these examples.

This level of pain, anger, and desperation is what can happen when we go through life keeping our problems a secret.

These women wrote me because I asked for their secrets, and you only respond to a request like that if your secret is a burden to you, and you need to let it out. The unhappiness in marriage is compounded and magnified by the fact that they've suffered alone and in silence for so many years. It breaks my heart. I want to hug every one of them and let them know that the first step to alleviating some of the crushing ache is to stop suffering alone.

---

## UNLOCKING THE SECRET

It's not a sin to be disappointed in marriage, unfulfilled by your spouse, or to want more out of life than what you have. It's no shame to say you don't enjoy being abused; there's nothing wrong with you if you desire a close, connected relationship with your spouse and are saddened that you don't have it.

So why are women carrying the secret of their marital disenchantment? I have a few ideas.

*They are feeling guilty for not being content with their lives.* Most of us, whether we have been brought up as Christians or not, have a strong sense that we are *supposed to be* grateful for what we have because there is always someone who has it worse. We feel guilty if we don't exhibit the proper gratitude for basics such as having a roof over our heads and food to eat. When it becomes apparent that something is making us very unhappy, the *mean mothers* in our heads kick in: *Why aren't you satisfied with what you have? You're so ungrateful.*

The fact is we think, feel, and desire because these are God-given abilities. Our thoughts, feelings, and desires speak to us about what we want. Even if our feelings are not reflecting the truth at that moment, their nagging existence shows us there is something that needs to be addressed in our lives. A pervasive feeling of unhappiness is an extremely important signal, either that our situation needs to change or that we need to learn a more healthy and productive response to our situation.

*They are feeling shame that their marriages aren't perfect when other marriages seem to be.* I mentioned in an earlier chapter that we tend to compare our insides to other people's outsides. We believe that other people's marriages are better than ours. The truth is we have no idea what it's like inside another marriage, and more often than not, things are not all rosy. But we feel shameful because we think we're the only ones who can't seem to make a marriage work. Also, many women—Christian or not—live by the taboo that it is not okay to talk negatively about your spouse or marriage. That it is not proper, it shows a lack of loyalty, and it makes you look like a complainer. Let me suggest that not talking about what is churning inside of you (to a caring friend or a professional of your choosing) may cause it to leak out in unexpected places. None of us can act well enough to hide everything forever.

Once you get real with others, and they start to get real with you, it becomes clear that the sense of shame over an imperfect marriage is misplaced. We all have imperfect marriages.

*They believe talking about it is futile or only makes it more difficult to endure. Talking doesn't fix anything, so why not just keep it to them-*

*selves?* It's easy to give in to hopelessness, convincing ourselves that no matter what we do, nothing will change. When we are experiencing something intense and all-consuming, our view of the situation is narrow and limited. We keep trying the same things over and over to solve our problem. We think we need to just try harder, and the idea of talking about it seems pointless. But the truth is that bringing issues into awareness and then sharing them with God and another safe person is the crucial first step for healing in almost any emotional, psychological, or relational situation.

*Bringing it out into the open means they have to face the problem and take action to do something about it.* Yes, this is true. And sometimes the idea of actually having to do the work of addressing the problems in marriage seems so overwhelming, scary, or impossible that our response is to try to keep it in the box, hoping the lid doesn't blow off someday. Taking action also means the possibility of unwanted change. Most women's lives aren't *all* bad, and getting a less-than-desirable outcome or being the only one making the changes in the face of an unwilling spouse is disheartening.

*They fear that rocking the boat will make things worse than they already are.* Sometimes we'd rather keep the status quo than upset things—no matter how unworkable the status quo is. We exist in a kind of inertia, having a natural tendency to prefer things as they are rather than take the risk of change. We are afraid something bad is going to happen. But something bad *is* happening; it's just happening slowly, and it's underground or unacknowledged. Rocking the boat could possibly make things worse for a time. Most people are resistant to change, any kind of change, especially at the prompting of another person. Often when someone is brave enough to attempt change, other family members work harder at getting back to that familiar status quo. But if you're committed to working toward a solution for your life and are willing for things to be less familiar and even uncomfortable for a time, things will eventually be better than they are now.

*They hope if they ignore it, the problem will get better or go away on its own.* No matter how many times we tell ourselves this isn't logical, we still talk ourselves into believing it. Our fear paralyzes us. A good example of this is Amy, an intelligent, professional woman who has been unhappy in her marriage for a long time. Her friends have brought it up, but she doesn't want to do anything about it, insisting her husband is going to see the light . . . eventually. But that's not how things work. Usually a situation left untended keeps getting worse until something blows up or somebody does something that destroys things on a much deeper level. Sure enough, this is what has happened in Amy's marriage. An infidelity has been revealed, and things have gotten much, much worse. Luckily, it's forced them into counseling. Sometimes things need to be upset in order to prompt change.

So all of these excuses we give ourselves for keeping secrets turn out to be faulty. That should tell us it's not such a great idea to keep our secrets in the first place. But are there any other reasons we should consider letting our secrets out?

## Keeping the Secret

Every situation is different. But in general, the deadliest thing about keeping your marriage difficulties secret is that it keeps you from being able to actively seek solutions. You may be so deep into sadness or despair over your situation that it seems hopeless. It feels as though *nothing* can be done, nothing will *ever* change. You become resigned. This is your fate. This must be God's will for your life . . . your cross to bear.

That's rarely the truth of a situation. No matter how desperate your situation seems, there are always options—there is always help available. One of the most insidious things the enemy does is to convince us that our problem is *different* from everyone else's—our problem is the one that can't be helped by counseling, that can't be helped by changing our actions, behaviors, responses, and attitudes. Ours is the one problem that resists solutions. We are doomed to live a miserable life, and there is nothing we can do about it. Think hard about this. Are you keeping your secret because you have been thinking this way? If so, I encourage you to reject the lies of the enemy and instead ask God to begin showing you the truth about your situation.

Another problem with keeping our marital disappointments a secret is that our pain grows. It's like an infection hidden in a dark environment where it can fester and multiply unhindered.

When you are deeply hurt and disappointed in your marriage but keeping it a secret, in the absence of other solutions, you'll naturally obsess or fantasize about getting out of the marriage. You skip over all the possible ways to deal with your situation and improve it. When the pain becomes bad enough that you're motivated to actually *do something* about the problem, the only thing that seems reasonable is to end the marriage altogether. For many, many reasons, divorce is not the best solution, and certainly not the only solution. But secret keeping and allowing our pain to expand to the point of becoming debilitating can make any other answer unthinkable.

One more downside to keeping all this to yourself: it doesn't allow you to connect with other women who might be experiencing something similar and might be able to help you. Revealing your weaknesses, fears, failures, and disappointments to another trusted person usually has the effect of drawing the person closer to you. Without that connection and a safe place to verbally process your pain, your secret becomes all the more painful.

## THINK ABOUT IT

Since this book is about the secrets women keep, and women keep secrets about every major issue in their lives, we are going to be talking about serious problems women face. Unhappiness in marriage is just one of them.

As a psychologist in clinical practice, my instinct and desire is to share with you pages and pages of principles—both psychological and spiritual—that can help you with each of these issues. However, that's not what this book is for. We'll only be addressing each issue as it relates to being a *secret*.

So while I'd love to write twenty more chapters about marriage and all the ways to try to make it work, I'm not going to. As you know, there are hundreds of books available to help you. There are marriage counselors, pastors, and church counselors available to help. I encourage you to seek out the kind of help you personally need. I'm not going to do an in-depth analysis of problem marriages and figure out how to fix yours. But I can give you some things to consider in thinking about what to do with this secret.

First, whatever your situation, no matter how deep your discontent, *your pain is real, and it deserves attention*. It is crying out to you, telling you that something is broken and needs to be fixed. You are in a difficult place, and I want you to know that I'm not minimizing it or suggesting there is anything easy about this. Just take what makes sense to you, and discard the rest.

Many women spend months and years trying to figure out how to get their spouses to respond to them, often to no avail: *If only my spouse would talk to me. If he were only romantic or social or engaging, or spent more time at home or didn't watch so much TV, or worked more or worked less. If we only had more common interests. If my partner only would love me the way I need to be loved, then I'd be okay.*

When your focus is on all the ways your husband isn't meeting your needs, it becomes more and more difficult to look at what's going on inside of *you*. The relationship is so all-consuming that it keeps you from knowing and exploring yourself and taking the time to consider what you could be doing to either change the situation or change your response to anything you can't change.

Susie is a highly successful executive who has spent years juggling marriage, motherhood, and a career. Her husband is a responsible man but doesn't particularly enjoy working and has never pursued a sizable income; consequently, while she yearns to slow down, go back to school, and be relieved of the responsibility to be the primary breadwinner, it hasn't happened and doesn't appear to be a possibility anytime soon. She is exhausted and becomes more and more frustrated with her husband as time goes by and things stay the same. She despairs over and over again: *When will he step up? When will he be what I need him to be?*

Susie's focus on her husband's failings keeps her from seeing a few important truths. Her husband is who he is—who he's always been. He may not ever change, and why should he? The system works for him. She's been equally responsible with him for creating this system. Unless she figures out how to change her expectations and accept her husband as he is, she will be constantly primed for disappointment, anger, and resentment. Over the years, she has trained her husband to accept her as the primary breadwinner, and she's made it clear to him that she thrives on her career. He has no reason to think she may have changed her mind about this arrangement. If she truly wants things to change, she is going to have to talk to him about it. Finally, she chose this man for reasons consciously and unconsciously having to do with the fact that his laid-back personality fit well with her efficient, take-charge qualities. This is an opportunity for her to explore what has changed and why she has kept up a facade for so long if it wasn't really who she was or what she wanted.

Susie says her secret is that she is resentful and angry with her husband all the time. But her deeper secret, the one she is having trouble admitting to herself, is that for years she's been allowing her husband to evade financial responsibility because it served her purposes—need for control, feeling of power, ego in being the breadwinner. Susie needs to look at the underlying issue, in order to be able to make changes in the happiness level of her marriage.

We naturally focus on our husbands, especially when there are problems. This is one of the consequences from the fall of Adam and Eve in the garden of Eden. Woman's curse was, in short, to be focused toward her husband while he was focused outward. Genesis 3:16–19 describes this when God told the woman that, along with pain in childbirth, "Your desire will be for your husband, and he will rule over you." And to Adam, God said, "Because you listened to your wife . . . cursed is the ground because of you. . . . By the sweat of your brow you will eat your food." I think God was the first to put tough love to work in order to save us from ourselves!

If we redirect our focus to ourselves, we are now in a territory where we can actually make things happen. Even if your husband is really the problem—let's say you're not exaggerating, and he's 90 percent of the issue—you can still focus on your own 10 percent: How am I contributing to the dynamic? How have I enabled and allowed it, and what am I doing to keep it going? Am I paying attention to who my husband really is and appreciating his good qualities?

It's easy to look at all the ways we *don't* have power in a relationship. We can't change another person, that's true. So instead, if we find the areas in which we have some power and control, we can choose to operate in those areas. We can control our responses. We can choose to live with integrity and seek God and do the best we can in every way, regardless of outside circumstances. That's where our power lies.

One way we all have some control is we can choose to talk honestly to our husbands about what we want and need and what's missing. Believe me, I know how difficult these conversations can be. I know husbands aren't always the most receptive listeners. But still, we can choose to try to make ourselves clear. When we're clear—unambiguous, firm—we have more power. When we stay vague, when we're wishy-washy and unwilling to stand firm in expressing our needs, we lose power. There is more strength in being *real* than trying to pretend in order to avoid conflict.

There may be something you really don't like about your spouse, but that might be who he is. You don't have to love everything about your husband, but you may want to consider the concept of acceptance. We choose to be honest about the other person's strengths and weaknesses, and be as accepting as possible of the whole person. We can also figure out ways to minimize the impact on ourselves of the things we don't like.

Often we are angry at the ways he doesn't measure up. We have to acknowledge our anger. We can't believe we ended up with somebody who isn't living up to our expectations. We think we were entitled to something different. But when we recognize the humanity of others, the very human imperfection we all struggle with, it can help us have more compassion and less resentment for the limitations of our husbands.

One of the reasons this is so difficult in marriage is that we are often looking for our mates to be more than human. We expect our husbands to make up for past wounds, to love and care for us in a way that is second only to God. In general, people tend to minimize their own faults and maximize those of others, as well as attributing malicious intent to others. Our disappointment in ourselves is hard to deal with—it's much easier to look at *his* faults. We can make excuses for ourselves or put our behavior in the context of making a mistake. After all, we didn't mean to act that way; we were just having a bad day. Even so, we might get frustrated with ourselves ("I can't believe I keep doing that!"). But we're much harder on our husbands when they don't behave as we think they should. ("He knows that that upsets me and did it anyway. He just ignores my feelings.")

A second thing I wanted to point out about unhappiness in marriage is this: perhaps constant happiness isn't the goal of marriage, and periods of unhappiness are normal and even healthy. Gary Thomas wrote a groundbreaking book about it, called *Sacred Marriage*. In it he asks, "What if God had an end in mind that went beyond our happiness, our comfort, and our desire to be infatuated and happy as if the world were a perfect place? *What if God designed marriage to make us holy more than to make us happy?*"[1]

It's something to consider.

## SPIRITUAL SECRETS

One thing that makes me sad when talking to women about marriage is when they feel trapped by the fact that they're Christians. They believe in the lifelong commitment they made, and they know

God hates divorce (Mal. 2:16), so they feel sentenced to the prison of their marriage.

If you're in this situation, please consider whether living a life of resentment and anger is really what God wants for you. Yes, I know God allows suffering in life. But I don't believe He created marriage for the purpose of causing suffering. In fact, I believe He created marriage as a sort of life raft in the ocean of life's suffering.

What if your marriage is not a life raft? What if, instead, your marriage threatens to drown you on a daily basis? I encourage you to take the steps in the next section and sincerely endeavor to change your perspective, your responses, or your situation.

While I don't advocate or accept divorce as the best solution for most marriages, and feel that marriage is worth fighting for, even against great odds, I also am aware that divorce happens and is sometimes unavoidable. In fact, in some extreme situations, it's the best option. But what breaks my heart is when well-intentioned Christians look at divorce as an unforgivable sin. I see people living in fear, living trapped in their misunderstanding of God's Word, living in desperate situations because they fear disappointing God if they even consider ending a marriage. This is difficult, but I want to suggest that maybe God doesn't just hate divorce; maybe it also breaks His heart when Christians sit with pain and anger and resentment for years, hopeless and helpless to change it. Resigning oneself to a trapped life is not marriage and leads to further despair. We can't control another person, but more times than not, our working at the relationship is only a varied repetition of same song, same dance. We do what we *know*, thinking we've done it all, while we are waiting for our spouses to change. I think perhaps God created marriage as a way to glorify Him; and if our marriages are not doing that, maybe we are obligated to do something about it.

Again, I'm not suggesting divorce as the answer. It is truly the last resort. I'm saying the smart thing to do is look at your situation honestly, explore every possible way of making it better, and ask yourself if there's any way possible to glorify God through your marriage. The next section will help you with that.

## From Secrets to Solutions

So how are we going to stop being burdened by secrets about our marriages? Remember, the goal is not to share your secret with the world but to strip it of its power, to stop allowing your secret to define you.

*Be honest with yourself.* Ask yourself, Why have I kept my problem marriage a secret? What's my part in this situation—what have I done to enable or continue it? What am I avoiding by not talking about this to anyone?

Perhaps the most important question to be asking is, What is the secret I'm hiding from myself? There are limitless possibilities, but you might be minimizing your own role in the unhappy marriage. You could be locked into a pattern of enabling your husband to continue behaviors that are unproductive or even destructive. Perhaps you and your husband haven't been in the habit of nurturing the marriage, so it has stagnated. Maybe you have baggage from your past that is impacting your marriage today. Whatever it is, try to be honest and uncover the secret behind the secret.

*Be honest with God.* Begin praying about your situation in a new way, asking God to open your eyes so you can see new ways to approach your marriage, to open your ears so that you can hear your husband in ways you haven't before. Look for your husband's heart in the midst of your heartache. Ask God for the wisdom to decide how to bring your secret out of the dark, and the courage to do it.

*Be honest with a therapist or other trained professional.* Whether you decide to get counseling right away—or whether you can afford it financially—a great step is to at least find one in your area, make a call, do the footwork, and get the information so you know where to turn when the time is right. Ask yourself if your relationship can afford *not* to receive help, or what the emotional costs will be in leaving things as they are. Ask at your church if they have marital counseling referrals. Look for a pastoral counselor whose primary role is marriage counseling, a licensed marriage and family therapist, a licensed clinical social worker, a clinical psychologist who does couples' work, or a psychiatrist who has a therapy practice (state to state, there are variations of titles and degrees of trained professionals). A professional who is Christian is preferable. If finances are truly the problem and not just a convenient excuse, then find out what they charge, whether your insurance covers it, whether you qualify for any discounts, and whether there are any free or low-cost clinics. After you have gathered the information, you can take your time deciding whether you want to follow up.

*Decide who else you can be honest with.* Do you have a best friend from whom you've been hiding your pain? Has your mother been asking you what's wrong, but you haven't wanted to tell her? Are you in a safe small group or Bible study in which you might share and ask for prayer?

With these steps, you can begin to neutralize the power this secret has over your life and move in the direction of healing your heart and finding something positive in your troubled marriage.

## Praying Scripture for Your Secret

Pray Isaiah 63:9.

Father in heaven, I know that in my suffering, You also suffer, and You have the power to personally rescue me. In Your love and mercy You will redeem me; You will lift me up and carry me through the years. Lord, help me to remember that You do not delight in my misery. I put my faith in You for rescue, trusting in Your mercy, thankful for Your unending love. Amen.

## Recommended Resources

*Boundaries in Marriage* by Henry Cloud and John Townsend
*Divorce Proofing Your Marriage: 10 Lies that Lead to Divorce and 10 Truths that Will Stop It* by Linda S. Mintle, PhD
*Every Woman's Marriage* by Shannon and Greg Ethridge
*How to Save Your Marriage Alone* by Dr. Ed Wheat

*How We Love* by Milan and Kay Yerkovich
*Love and Respect* by Emerson Eggerichs
*Redemptive Divorce: A Biblical Process that Offers Guidance for the Suffering Partner, Healing for the Offending Spouse, and the Best Catalyst for Restoration* by Mark W. Gaither
*Sacred Marriage* by Gary Thomas

# Chapter 5

# I've Had an Emotional or Physical Affair

Carol is a prominent member of a large, dynamic church and has been a Christian for many years. She's married, has children, and has worked hard to maintain a fruitful walk with the Lord. In fact, she'd been feeling especially close to God and was excited by new truths she'd learned in her Bible study when she found herself alone in an office with her pastor, a man she'd long respected and admired. Their discussion turned personal, and soon the pastor was telling her how beautiful she was and how he'd been struggling with being attracted to her.

That tiny spark proved irresistible to Carol, who, like many of us, craved the attention and appreciation of a man. Her heart fell instantly, and as the pastor moved in to kiss her, she instinctively responded. This was the beginning of an affair that, so far, has stopped just short of intercourse but has included nearly everything else. These two believers in Christ are in contact several times a day through e-mail, text messages, phone calls, and frequent in-person meetings. A stolen kiss, a forbidden touch, sometimes more, then back to their separate spouses, their separate lives. She knows it's wrong, but in his arms she feels more alive and attractive than she has in years.

Carol feels as if she is on a roller coaster of emotion. One minute the tantalizing thrill electrifies her body, and then the shocking shame feels as if she's completely lost herself. She literally doesn't recognize the person behaving this way, yet she can't seem to break free. The knowledge of her sin, of who she's become, devastates her. She turns to God's Word and knows she needs to stop, but no matter how many times she tries to break it off, it never works. She can't resist his advances. She prays for release from these feelings, and she wonders if she'll ever find herself again. Carol wonders whether this has ever happened to anyone else . . . or if she's the only Christian who's ever behaved this way.

Maybe this scenario is completely foreign to you. Maybe you couldn't imagine it in a million years. For your sake, I hope that's true. But Carol never imagined it either. It took her by surprise, and by the time she actually faced what she was doing, it was too late. She was caught in the web and unable to free herself.

Sadly, this situation is far from unusual. Carol fears she is alone in her struggle, but the truth is, sexual and emotional infidelity are going on everywhere—inside the church and out. The fact that it's the ultimate betrayal and has to do with sex makes it one of the deepest, darkest secrets women keep.

A large number of women wrote in to the Secrets Blog, sharing the stories of their infidelity.

> Four years ago, as a pastor's wife with no intimacy in my marriage, I fell into an emotional affair with a man at my church. This was something that I never thought was possible, and neither did anyone who knew me. For years I had silently struggled with lack of sexual intimacy and little attention being paid to my needs. Who was I going to talk to about this? No one. I never thought it would

come to an affair, but when it happened, it met many of my unmet needs. A whole lot of pain later, I have repented and accepted responsibility for my actions. My husband is no longer in the ministry and has accepted responsibility for his part in what happened.

✦ ✦ ✦

I had an affair on my husband of almost ten years. He was a good man and worked two jobs to make ends meet. To make things worse, I was a born-again, Spirit-filled believer when this happened! I was totally backslidden and living for myself. I still live with a tremendous amount of guilt even though I know God has forgiven me completely. The Bible says, "All things work together for good to them that love God and are called according to His purpose," but I have been so ashamed of the way I acted that I have not been able to tell many people.

The devastation to marriages and lives because of affairs is staggering. There are few things that hurt more than having your partner cheat on you. If you're the betrayer, there is hardly anything more shame provoking and seemingly unforgivable than sexually straying. And the culture we live in makes sexual attraction so easy that it can be nearly impossible for some people to resist.

Men and women work closely together in offices, churches, hospitals, and every other possible location. E-mail, instant messaging, text messaging, and cell phones make immediate and constant contact easy. Marriages are faltering with partners not having enough time or paying enough attention to each other, so people are lonely and vulnerable.

And on top of all this—or perhaps creating all of this—is the enemy, no doubt rubbing his hands together in glee as we fall into his carefully set traps. He is having a field day with us as he makes temptation and sin irresistible, and when we keep our secrets and suffer in our shame, he is accomplishing his purpose: "The thief comes only to steal and kill and destroy" (John 10:10). He is out to steal our joy in salvation, to kill our devoted attention to the Lord, and to destroy the full life that Jesus intends for us.

But we can't rest on "the devil made me do it." We can't use spiritual warfare as our excuse. Yes, the devil tempts us at our point of weakness, and yes, spiritual warfare is real. But we are responsible for our behavior.

---

## Unlocking the Secret

The defining characteristic of an affair is not whether there is sex involved, but the concealment that surrounds it and the fact that someone is being betrayed.

In *Anatomy of a Secret Life*, Dr. Gail Saltz wrote, "What defines an affair isn't sex but secrecy. A deep exchange of secrets serves as the foundation for intimacy, and such intimacy *can* lead to sex. But it can also lead to a nonsexual but equally compelling and consuming relationship: an emotional affair."[1]

An emotional affair can be just as destructive as a physical affair since it engages the heart and mind and typically involves a level of intimacy far beyond that of a friend and sometimes greater than the intimacy in a marriage. It entails the same level of bondage as a physical affair, the sort of addiction effect that illicit relationships carry. The person is aware of doing something gravely wrong and hurtful while simultaneously recognizing that she also feels happier than she has in a long time. The giddy feelings, the emotional rush of being appreciated and admired, and the "in love" feeling are so intoxicating that people lose their ability to control their behavior. They are addicted almost as if they'd been smoking crack cocaine.

I believe affairs, both emotional and physical, are almost as widespread among Christians as in the general population, although more believers might engage in the emotional variety, fooling themselves into thinking the affair is okay if it doesn't involve skin. It's easier to compartmentalize the affair when it's not overtly sexual, going along convincing yourself that it really doesn't have anything to do with real life. But the betrayal is just as real. An emotional affair means someone besides your husband has become your confidant, and that's not only a supreme betrayal of your husband, but it reeks of disrespect for him as a person.

If you have any sort of secret relationship going on, any behavior that you're not willing to share with your husband, this is a huge red flag that something is wrong.

## KEEPING THE SECRET

Some women wrote me with sad tales of carrying guilt for a long-ago, long-over affair for which they can't forgive themselves. Some had a brief dalliance or one-night stand; others had a long-standing adulterous relationship. Some women are still in the clutches of their affairs—either unwilling or unable to let them go. Some have had their affairs revealed publicly; some have confessed to their husbands while others have never been found out and have never shared the information with anyone, not even their spouses.

> I live with a very dark secret. I had an affair with a man I thought was everything I ever wanted in a man but didn't get with the man I married. I almost gave up everything for him—but he didn't turn out to be the man he said he was. I must now carry this with me the rest of my life. I have asked for forgiveness from God but cannot or will not tell my husband. I do not keep it a secret because I'm afraid for myself, but for the pain it would bring my husband. He does not deserve the pain that I caused because of my stupidity and weakness.

In talking about the secrets of affairs, we need to address who we're keeping secrets from. The most important issue, of course, is your marriage. Has your affair been found out, or have you confessed to your husband?

Therapists vary in their advice on this point, and most are pretty adamant about their particular stance. I want to say first that every affair situation is different, every marriage is different, and the individuals are carrying different baggage from their past that will affect how they move forward. Having said that, I believe it's unhealthy to keep the affair a secret from your husband. He deserves to know the truth in order to be able to process reality and make decisions for himself accordingly. As we've discussed, there is power in truth—although in this case, the truth can be the most dreadful blow the person has ever received. Yet the truth is the one avenue toward true healing.

If you continue to keep your affair to yourself, even though it may be over, there is an ongoing secret in your marriage. You've had an experience that your husband didn't have. There's a profound disconnect between you that may never be bridged. Keeping the secret *keeps the affair alive*.

## THINK ABOUT IT

We all want to be loved. In this world full of brokenness—broken hearts, broken dreams, broken marriages—we can be tempted to take love wherever we find it, even if it's a counterfeit love. The drive to be loved is so strong that it can overrule your concern for the feelings of a spouse or your concern for your children, your job, or your Christian walk.

So when you think you've found that love you've been missing, of course you keep it a secret. Being found out would certainly change things in your life. And sometimes you just don't want to be found out because you don't want it to end. It may feel as if it were the first time you've ever been understood, or maybe it was the most powerful relationship you've ever had. You rationalize that you had genuine needs that weren't being fulfilled in your marriage. You were caught off guard by the affair and never meant for it to happen, so it's not as though you were *trying* to hurt anyone.

But keeping the secret does not lead to healing; neither will it lead to a restored and renewed relationship with God. Recovering from an affair is a long and arduous process and could be the most difficult thing you've ever done—whether you are the betrayer or the betrayed. Many people are surprised when two, five, or eight years have passed and they still don't feel completely over it. But the path to healing begins with the first step, and here is a simple outline of how to get started unloading the secret.

*Recognize you're in an affair or had one in the past.* Admit it to yourself and face the truth of where you are. Seek out a counselor to begin working through the process of accountability and repentance. Decide with your counselor how and when to confess the affair to your spouse.

*Remove the temptation from your life.* Get away from the temptation, no matter how difficult this is. Don't negotiate with it. The Bible says to "flee from sexual immorality" (1 Cor. 6:18). Do whatever it takes—a new job, a new e-mail address, a new cell phone number. You can't have true healing if you are still in contact with the person you had the affair with. Treat that relationship like cancer, in need of immediate surgery to remove it from your life. It's that serious.

*Reconnect with your spouse.* This isn't going to be smooth; in fact, reconnecting with your husband will probably feel terrible at the beginning. You got all these really good feelings from your affair, and you're not going to get good feelings right away in the reconnection process. But don't give up. Make sure you have the support of a counselor and possibly an accountability group and/or a few good friends who can walk you through it.

*Resist the urge to make excuses for yourself, blaming your husband for your affair.* The appropriate time will come for you two to address the ways you both contributed to a situation in which there was not a great deal of intimacy. But first you must take responsibility for your actions, demonstrate your genuine remorse and repentance, and do whatever it takes to help your husband heal and to make sure it never happens again.

Of course, this is a vastly simplified explanation. Hundreds of pages have been written to help people recover from affairs (see the list of books at the end of the chapter). Here, my purpose is to help you recognize that *there is relief* from the secret burdening you, even if it takes years to truly experience peace. You might as well start now.

## SPIRITUAL SECRETS

If you've been keeping your affair a secret, it might help you to be reminded that confession can be the catalyst for the greatest change you've ever experienced in your marriage—a change for the better. Yes, it most likely will deeply wound the people you love. It might have consequences beyond your control, such as your husband being unable to consider staying in the marriage. But as the book *After the Affair* puts it, "You may in time come to see the affair not merely as a regrettable trauma but as an alarm, a wake-up call. You may eventually discover that you needed a nuclear explosion like an affair to blow your previous construction apart and allow a healthier, more conscious and mature version to take its place."[2]

As you open up the truth of who you are, you will have the opportunity to experience the love of Jesus in a way you never knew before. You'll be able to understand the incomprehensible grace of God in an entirely new way. You'll see exactly what forgiveness means when you need it as never before but can do nothing to earn it. I encourage you to use this time to draw closer to God, to seek first His kingdom and His righteousness, to cast yourself on His mercy and accept His healing touch on your life.

I'm always moved whenever I read the story in John 8 about the woman caught in adultery. Jesus didn't make light of her sin, yet His words to her were so tender: "Go now and leave your life of sin" (v. 11). He must have already known she had a repentant heart. She didn't need to be beaten up or verbally chastised—she was probably doing a good job of that in her own mind. But He needed to let her know that her choices from here on out would matter. *Leave your life of sin.* Change directions. Change everything if you have to. But leave this sin behind.

You've got a choice, and you have numerous resources available to support you in your choice. I encourage you to make the choice toward freedom.

## FROM SECRETS TO SOLUTIONS

Janette and Iris were business acquaintances who met for lunch occasionally. It was only when Janette hinted one day that she'd been having an extended e-mail relationship with a man that Janette and Iris's friendship deepened. Iris, shocked by Janette's revelation, admitted she was involved in the very same thing. This led them to long, deep conversations about the state of their lives, the shame of their sin, and how to break free of these affairs. They each became the other's closest confidante about the hidden side of their lives.

During the next several years, that honesty served them well. Together they were able to process the feelings as they navigated the difficult terrain of confession, accountability, repentance, and marital restoration. Because they've each had that one safe place to be real, neither has suffered from feeling burdened with a secret but instead has used the friendship as a catalyst for true healing. Years later, when either of them experiences any kind of emotional fallout from their long-ago affair, they are still able to process it within the friendship. The fact that they love and accept each other fully, even knowing everything about each other's darkest side, has been an important factor in their healing and ongoing emotional stability.

Beryl Singleton Bissell wrote, "I believe the Church has done a great disservice in not placing its greatest emphasis on God's unconditional love, for if we realized how God loves us, we would recuperate from our falls much more quickly. How many turn away from God because of guilt, because their sense of unworthiness convinces them they cannot change?"[3]

Your confession is your path to beginning to understand God's unconditional love. It is the way to be relieved of the burden of your secret and your guilt.

*Be honest with yourself.* Your secret might be your affair, but maybe there's another secret you're keeping, even from yourself. Maybe it's your unhappy marriage. Maybe it's a long-standing pattern of needing affirmation from men. Maybe you are still devastated from never having a father's love. Whatever it is, get honest with yourself about why you were vulnerable to an affair in the first place.

*Be honest with God.* God has seen this all before. An affair is nothing new to Him, so don't be afraid to go to Him and throw yourself on His mercy. Lay it out there. Confess. And even if you haven't extricated yourself yet, begin praying fervently for the strength and wisdom to do so.

A novelist friend wrote, "You know, David was called a man after God's own heart, not because he got it right all the time, but because he desired to get it right all the time. I believe the Lord gave us that example to show us that's all He asks of any of us."[4] Do you desire to get it right for God? Go to Him and tell Him about it.

*Be honest with a counselor.* Talk to a counselor or an accountability group or a trusted friend. Don't think you're going to make it through this alone. Keeping the secret locked up inside will keep you a slave to it. Let it out, and seek wise counsel about your every step from here on.

*Be honest with your husband.* I can't promise any particular result from confessing the affair to your spouse. I wish I could, but you are already aware of the deep pain this will cause. As my friend Kay Yerkovich wrote, "Confessing a secret or a lie might be one of the hardest things you ever do. It could cost you your marriage, but it isn't much of a marriage when you have to pretend."[5] Trust God to pick up the pieces of your heart, your marriage, and your family. He is a forgiving God. "His anger lasts only a moment, but his favor lasts a lifetime" (Ps. 30:5). He is waiting for you to turn to Him and toward the rest of your life. This is not an easy road, but it is the path to freedom.

## Praying Scripture for Your Secret

Pray 1 John 1:9.

Lord Jesus, if I confess my sins, You are faithful and just and will forgive my sins and purify me from all unrighteousness. Thank You for Your forgiveness, Lord. Please help me to stop hiding my sin and to confess it in the appropriate way, and help me to accept Your forgiveness. Purify me, Lord, and help me to move forward with You, in the light of Your love. Amen.

## Recommended Resources

Marriage Builders—www.marriagebuilders.com

### Books
*After the Affair* by Janis Abrahms Spring, PhD
*Anatomy of a Secret Life* by Gail Saltz, MD
*Confessions of a Good Christian Girl* by Tammy Maltby
*Every Woman's Battle* by Shannon Ethridge and Stephen Arterburn
*Surviving an Affair* by Willard F. Harley Jr. and Jennifer Chalmers Harley
*Torn Asunder* by Dave Carder

# Chapter 6

## My Partner Uses Pornography or Has Had an Affair

Lisa and Dave have been married for twenty years. In the early part of their marriage, Lisa began to find pornographic magazines in the house, and although she expressed her displeasure, it didn't change Dave's behavior. Soon she started finding XXX videos. She confronted Dave but to no avail. She didn't protest too loudly—she didn't want to put the marriage at risk.

When everyone started getting the Internet in their homes, Dave couldn't wait to jump on board. Lisa was completely against it, but her protests were ignored. Now they have not only the unlimited supply of porn that the Internet pipes in, but Lisa has found CDs and jump drives with thousands of pornographic images and video clips.

Lisa constantly feels nauseated and nervous, and she says her worry over Dave's porn use "controls her every waking moment." She wishes Dave could understand how much it hurts her, and that he *is* cheating. She says Dave won't go to a counselor and discourages her from going too. Lisa feels as though she can't talk to her pastor, and she has nowhere to turn. She feels as if the life is being slowly sucked out of her, and she needs help.

+ + +

Julie and Ron have been married for fifteen years. Three years ago Ron had an affair. Julie found out, but Ron never apologized, nor did he examine himself or his motivations or make any attempt to seek counseling. No one else knows about the affair, and Julie hasn't spoken with anyone because she doesn't feel as though it's her secret to tell—she doesn't want to be a gossip. Julie also feels great shame over Ron's affair as if she were responsible because of her failure as a wife. Julie and Ron have three children, and she tries to keep the peace so that their environment stays secure. Ron provides for their material needs but is cold and distant. Julie feels as if she is counting the days until her children are old enough for her to leave Ron. Until then, she feels that she is being held hostage.

Both Lisa and Julie have been betrayed. While having an affair versus being a habitual porn addict are different behavior manifestations, the devastation suffered by the two wives is much the same. They feel devalued, unloved, cast aside. Betrayal cuts a woman to her core. She is angry and resentful. She feels like a failure. And she is ashamed.

So she might be keeping it a secret.

When women keep secrets about their husbands' betrayals, they are being complicit in their behavior. They are allowing and even encouraging the behavior through their silence, and their shame grows because deep inside they know they're letting themselves down. They know they're not standing up for what's right.

Women keep secrets about their partners' affairs or pornography even when they're not married. Boyfriends and fiancés sometimes betray women as well, and many of us stay silent and stay involved just as we would if we were married.

My heart breaks for Lisa and Julie and every other woman who has been the victim of such unfaithfulness. I want to share with you the idea that healing can come from revealing the secret. In fact, you might discover that this is not even *your* secret to keep.

---

## Unlocking the Secret

Many women experience betrayal at the hands of their partners in the form of an affair or a pornography addiction—but not all women keep it a secret. Some women are the opposite: as soon as they find out, they're on the phone with their girlfriends and calling their mothers and making appointments with counselors. They're not about to put up with this! The women who keep it to themselves have strong reasons for doing so, and as you can tell from reading their letters, they have a lot in common.

> I am engaged to a man who had a sexual addiction/porn problem. I called off our wedding because he "slipped" and "peeked" at a porn site. Transsexual porn! He cheated on me with two cross-dressers and a friend of mine. Everything came out because I backed him up against the wall with the truth in my hands . . . and then he admitted everything. He has since turned his life over to God and joined a men's group. He has connected with men in our church. We have now been together five years. He loves God, has incredible faith, and does this walk with Christ so beautifully. There are many at church that know our struggles and are just so amazed at the transformation in our lives. We live together and do not have sex because we

wanted to start over "right" in God's eyes. He is in the Word, and he is so changed.

But the truth is, I am full of rage. He's transformed—but I am repulsed. I cry all the time, alone. My pain is so, so deep. When everyone is around us, I pretend I'm happy, that we are so happy, that God is so amazing (which He is). But I am broken inside. I trust nothing anymore . . . except for God, and He is not taking all this away, and that makes me angry too. I am smiling on the outside and dying on the inside. I hate being so sad but can't get out of all this pain. And nobody really knows because I don't want to make anyone feel uncomfortable. My pastor just loves to be around me because of all my good energy . . . as does everyone. I am such a delight to be around. I just want to vomit!

✦ ✦ ✦

Currently, my deepest and darkest secrets are actually my husband's. I keep his thirty-year addiction to porn a secret. I have sat silently in three different counselor's offices, listening to him lie about it or minimize it, always hoping he would own up to it. I keep my concerns about my sanity secret as well. He is very good with words and manipulation, and I get confused in the chaos and pain. In order to keep quiet, I have isolated myself from most friends and family. I avoid contact with the outside world as much as humanly possible.

✦ ✦ ✦

My husband has been having an affair for more than two years with a woman at his job. I found out with definite proof about a year ago. He continues to connect with her, and I have stood by him, but my heart aches, and I am beyond depressed all the time. I am a good wife, but I feel completely and utterly alone, and I will never be happy and confident again.

+ + +

I have been married eighteen years, and we have three children together. I recently discovered that my husband had an affair with a nineteen-year-old past employee who my children and I have known very well for four years. The worst part is that she gave birth to a son who is my husband's child. He doesn't know that I know, but I read his e-mail and found out. Now I'm devastated and don't know what to do. I don't want my marriage to end. I still love him even though I hate him and have thoughts of hurting her and myself.

If you're anything like me, you find these letters heartbreaking. There is so much pain in being alone. You can hear it in the women's anguished words how their sense of isolation makes the devastation all the more hideous. But there are a couple of reasons I wanted you to see these examples of this terrible secret women keep. First, the women who wrote me deserve a chance to be heard. I want them to know that their stories matter to us, that we hear them, and we want to help. Second, I want you to see the evidence for yourself—the clearly disastrous effects of keeping such a secret.

Are you keeping the secret of your partner's infidelity? Please keep reading, and let me help you understand why it should be a secret no longer.

## KEEPING THE SECRET

Why do women keep these secrets? Why not expose their husbands and insist they change? Obviously there's a lot at stake. Most women don't want to lose their marriages. Others fear their marriages won't end but will become a living nightmare as their husbands refuse to change and become even more distant, cruel, or even violent. Women who have children will often go to great lengths to preserve the family home, something I'm not about to criticize, but they may be avoiding looking at the cost of such a decision.

There's fear involved in keeping the secret. *What will people think if this becomes public? What if my husband loses his job and can't support us—or what if he leaves and I have no way to support the family?*

Christian women may find it even more difficult if they think they're not allowed to speak up. A faithful woman may not say anything because, as Tammy Maltby puts it, "she wants to please God—and because she believes God wants her to submit to anything her husband dishes out . . . or she hopes her suffering will redeem him . . . or she has prayed for him to change and expects her prayers to be answered. She may be convinced it's God's will for families to stay intact no matter what or that she should forgive wrongs again and again."[1]

When a partner commits a sexual sin, the impetus to keep it a secret is even stronger because of what *we think* it says about *us*. Best-selling Christian recording artist Clay Cross and his wife, Renee, wrote compellingly about their struggle to heal after Clay's pornography addiction was revealed. Renee is a beautiful woman and a dedicated wife and mother. She relates:

> My first thought was *Where did I fail?* Even though he told me over and over that the problem had nothing to do with me, his reassurances didn't help. I felt inadequate as a woman. "Aren't you satisfied with me? What more could I have possibly done? If you have great sex every day, how could that not be enough?" I wanted to know. Some days I would stand in front of the mirror and wonder why he would want to look at other women. I wondered if I should have dressed in a different way or maybe cut my hair short

or grown it longer. I would turn to the side and wonder if I hadn't lost enough weight after our girls were born. Self-doubt overwhelmed me. *Something must be wrong with me.*[2]

Other women have experienced the same roller coaster of emotions as they wrestle with questions of *why* and come to the conclusion that their husbands' problems were actually *their* fault.

Women also keep their husbands' sexual sins a secret out of fear that others won't understand how deeply they hurt. It may seem as if others can easily brush off a man's attraction to porn (boys will be boys, after all), and our culture does everything to normalize this behavior. Thus, although the husband is committing a grievous betrayal against his wife, *she's the one who feels crazy.* And it's common for women to feel uncomfortable going to their pastors—other men, usually.

In their book *Every Heart Restored*, about healing from a husband's sexual sin, Fred and Brenda Stoeker wrote:

> Sadly, we've found that even pastors may struggle to fully understand the effects of sexual sin upon a wife's emotions, and even they can inadvertently make a woman feel a bit silly for even bringing the matter up. . . . [They] can have a peculiar blind spot when it comes to the sexual sins of porn and visual lust. When pastors counsel thieves, they don't suggest seeking out an accountability partner. Instead, they expect the guilty party to knock it off.[3]

But all too often, there's nobody telling a porn or sex-addicted husband to just *stop it.*

## THINK ABOUT IT

There are several tremendously helpful books written for those suffering from their partners' sexual sin, and I'll give you some recommendations at the end of the chapter. Right now I'm going to give you a few quick things to think about if you're keeping the secret of your husband's affair or porn addiction.

*It's not your fault.* When you've been betrayed, of course, you feel it's about *you* even though people may tell you it's not. *You* were the one betrayed. *You* are the one who's hurting. You weren't important enough in his heart and mind to prevent this. You may intellectually understand it wasn't about you, but your experience is that it's most definitely about you.

That's okay. If this is how you feel, please know that it's normal.

Yet please hear me when I say *you didn't cause it.* Nobody can force anyone else to fall into sexual sin. If there is a problem in the marriage, both people most likely contributed—yet if you've been betrayed, it's not your fault. Nothing you did or didn't do entitled your partner to have an affair or use pornography. That was his choice to handle his desires (or frustrations or whatever) in a selfish way outside of the marital relationship. Plenty of people have problems in marriage, yet their spouses don't cheat on them. You can't cause someone to have an affair.

Your husband may try to blame you, claiming you are cold or sexually distant or unresponsive. So how did you *expect* him to get his needs met? But listen to me: even if all those things were true, it's still not a valid rationalization. It still wouldn't give him the right to do what he did.

He may talk about how he's a man, he's visually oriented, and he has sexual needs that weren't being met. It doesn't matter. It is his responsibility to discipline himself or to get help if he can't.

As Drs. Henry Cloud and John Townsend wrote in *Boundaries in Marriage,* "An act of unfaithfulness is something that one person does, not two. . . . God does not become unfaithful if we do not love him correctly. He remains faithful no matter what we do. Marriage requires this as well."[4] Even if it's true that you did not love your husband correctly, you did not cause him to sin.

*It's okay to be angry.* In fact, something is wrong if you're not angry because it means you're not facing the reality of what's happened. If you've been keeping the secret of your husband's infidelity, you're most likely a cauldron of swirling hot emotions on top of anger. You're probably crushed by the loss of your dreams and the feeling of not being loved. You may feel like a fool, that you've been had. You probably have some guilt that you weren't *enough* of a wife to stop this from happening. And you most likely have some depression, on and off, ranging from medium to debilitating.

This is a lot to be dealing with, and it's no wonder the women who wrote me had such desperation in their voices. There is no way to deal with this level of emotional devastation on your own. You are angry—that's okay. You've got to let it out in some kind of healthy environment, which I'm going to talk about more on the following pages. The important thing to remember is that your anger is normal and healthy, and you can use that anger to help you take the steps you need to get out of this prison of silence and onto a road of healing.

*It's time to stop protecting him and to stand up for what's right.* This is a hard one. If standing up to him were easy, you wouldn't be keeping his secrets. You may love him, or you may be afraid of him, or you may be afraid of what life will be like without him. But know this: by keeping your husband's secrets, you are not helping him. You are simply allowing him to continue in a life of sin, and a lot of people are going to pay the price.

There's absolutely no hope of healing if you keep it inside! This problem will not go away. Your anger will never subside. He won't change his behavior. Keeping the secret dooms you to the "same old" until something explodes—and that will most likely be you.

Drs. Cloud and Townsend put it this way:

> There are the people in difficult situations who, because of
> some odd teaching or their own weaknesses, have not taken
> the stand they need to take against hurt or evil in their
> marriage. They have been too afraid or too guilty to stand
> up to abuse, irresponsibility, control, or other behavior that

destroys love. As a result, the behavior and their hurt have
continued. Then they . . . discover that God takes a stand
for what is good. God stands up for love and against evil.
God stands up for responsibility and freedom and against
domination and control. And they join God in the fight
for what is good. They set boundaries against evil and protect good things, like love and respect. And, as a result of
taking a courageous stance, their marriage is turned around
and saved.[5]

I can't promise you that your marriage will be saved, but I can
tell you I've seen many cases where marriages have survived and
thrived after betrayal was revealed and dealt with. On the other
hand, a marriage in which sin is kept under the rug will continue to
deteriorate and cause misery all around.

*Healing will require compassion, mercy, and understanding.* When
you decide to let your secret out of the bag, confront your husband,
and bring in a counselor or pastor, your anger will be so fresh and
raw that you really don't care to *understand* him. You have no compassion for him; in fact, the most you can muster is disgust.

But as time goes by, if you and your husband decide to try
restoring the marriage, your compassion for him will be necessary.
As he explores his own motivations and reveals the pain that led him
to this place, a bit of mercy from your side of the table will go a long
way in helping the restoration process. When you genuinely try to
understand some of what happened, it will finally help *you* because
you will learn that he never set out to intentionally hurt you. You'll
experience the knowledge that as much as it hurts, it really wasn't,
after all, about you. Even the relief in that knowledge may also have
a backhanded bite, in that it wasn't about you—and you're wanting
something, anything, to be about you in his eyes.

*Not all marriages get restored.* The fact that not all marriages
survive may seem obvious, but sometimes we need to hear it to
understand and accept the reality that the outcome isn't entirely in

our hands. Sometimes the hurt is too deep to be recovered from; sometimes the betrayer isn't willing to give up the object of his affection (whether it's another person or a series of photographic images). You can fight for your marriage, which is the right thing to do. But sometimes there comes a point when you realize you're fighting in vain. Please hear me when I say that *God still loves you.* He honors your heart and your intentions, He knows your limitations, and "His compassions never fail" (Lam. 3:22).

*You can choose hope for the future.* If you are working on rebuilding your marriage, it won't go anywhere without hope. You may have moments when your hope plays tug-of-war with your rage, and that's okay. But keep feeding your hope, and give your rage safe places to disburse. Read the stories of couples who have made it. Replace fear with total trust in the Lord. And look to the good in your husband, drawing it out every chance you get. As Brenda Stoeker said, "Choosing hope for the future is the first step to your freedom. Yes, even if your husband hasn't fully repented yet."[6] Whether or not your partner ever repents . . . whether your future is with him or without him . . . choose hope.

## Spiritual Secrets

Brenda Stoeker wrote in *Every Heart Restored* about the ways her faith in God was not only tested but pulled her through the crisis of her husband's sexual sin. Renee Cross echoed the same theme in *I Surrender All.* This is one of those times in life when you're going to need all the strength you can get just to make it through each day. Stand on your faith. Trust God for the outcome of this journey, no matter where it takes you.

Probably one of the most difficult things you will face, as mentioned previously, is finding compassion and mercy for your husband. I encourage you to pray for it daily and to grab hold of the tiny sparks of understanding that flit your way. Cultivate humility; after all, we're all sinners. Your journey of forgiveness will most likely be a long one, with fits and starts, ups and downs. You will think you've forgiven him and then find yourself angry again. You will process this over and over again. I've always thought Jesus said we were to forgive seventy times seven not only in reference to someone sinning against us multiple times, but because He knew that with some offenses, such as sexual betrayal, we have to keep extending forgiveness over and over again to the same person for the same hurt (Matt. 18:22).

You'll have to discipline yourself, just as your husband is learning discipline. You refuse to let despair take you down, and you trust that God is bringing you to a good place. "'For I know the plans I have for you,' declares the LORD, 'plans to prosper you and not to harm you, plans to give you hope and a future'" (Jer. 29:11). Thank God for His plans for you, and commit to following Him.

## FROM SECRETS TO SOLUTIONS

Giving up this secret might make things more difficult in the short term, but honestly, isn't almost anything better than the torture you've been under? Letting the air out of this secret will finally be the one thing that allows hope back into your life. Sharing it will give God and others a chance to help you toward healing.

*Be honest with yourself.* Explore the reasons you're keeping your partner's sexual sin a secret. Make a list of all your fears and your rationale. Then ask yourself, What is the secret I'm keeping from myself? What part of this am I trying not to face? Maybe it's your deep insecurities about your worth as a person and a wife, or about your appearance. Maybe you're most afraid of being embarrassed among your friends or church community. Whatever it is, you'll have more insight into the situation when you become honest with yourself about it.

*Be honest with God.* Cry out to God with your fears, your anger, and your disappointment in Him for allowing this to happen. He can handle it, I promise! He wants you to be real with Him as David was in the Psalms:

How long, O LORD? Will you forget me forever?
How long will you hide your face from me?
How long must I wrestle with my thoughts
and every day have sorrow in my heart?
How long will my enemy triumph over me? (Ps. 13:1–2)

Trust God with all the wounded parts of yourself, and over time, your faith and persistence will begin to melt your pain.

*Be honest with a counselor.* I can hardly overemphasize the importance of getting counseling if you've been betrayed in this way. The best scenario is if you and your partner go together, but if that's not possible, go alone. It's going to take a lot of work to get through the forgiveness process, and you need a safe place to air it all out. You'll need to look at what went wrong in the relationship and have help identifying areas in which you could improve. If you two are in counseling together, you'll need to discuss how to go about protecting your marriage and how to build a type of intimacy that is satisfying to both of you.

## PRAYING SCRIPTURE FOR YOUR SECRET

Pray 1 Corinthians 2:9.

Lord, You said that no eye has seen, no ear has heard, no mind has conceived what You have prepared for those who love You. I do love You, Lord, and I ask You to give me the hope of what You have in store for me. Help me trust the plans You have for me, no matter how desolate I feel right now. Lift me up from this dark place, take the weight of my secret from me, and bring me to the place You have prepared for me. Amen.

## RECOMMENDED RESOURCES

*Every Heart Restored* by Fred and Brenda Stoeker with Mike Yorkey
*Every Woman's Marriage* by Shannon and Greg Ethridge

*I Surrender All* by Clay and Renee Cross

*Not "Just Friends"* by Shirley P. Glass, PhD, with Jean Coppock
    Staeheli

*The Dance of Restoration* by Abel Ortega and Melodie Fleming

*Chapter 7*

# Being Single Was Not My Dream

I behave in ways that tell people I don't need men in my life. Having been hurt by men makes it hard for me to trust them, and living alone for many years makes them seem unnecessary, even though my secret goal is to be married.

✦ ✦ ✦

I'm terrified of marriage. It seems that even in the best of marriages, it's almost not worth the trouble. Your spouse could turn out to be crazy or abusive or just emotionally immature, and I don't trust myself to be able to detect any of those qualities before marriage. As much as I want that deep connection and someone to share my joys and burdens, I'm afraid it won't be worth it.

✦ ✦ ✦

After nine years of being divorced, I wonder if God really has someone out there for me. What will it take to find that true spiritual mate? Will my strong-willed attitude toward life make him run the other way?

✦ ✦ ✦

I'm afraid I will be single for the rest of my life.

In the previous chapters we addressed secrets that primarily affect married women, but I don't want you to think this book is only for wives. Although it sometimes *feels* as if almost everyone is married—we live in a couples-oriented society, and the Christian church is notoriously married-friendly—the truth is that the numbers of married and single American women are remarkably close. Actual figures vary, but one recent Census Bureau survey found 63 million married women and 54 million single women.[1]

You may have heard about studies indicating some women are happier unmarried, but it doesn't erase the truth that being single holds its own potential for emotional, financial, and logistical land mines. Some of them are no secret; for example, we're frequently hearing statistics that show women's socioeconomic status dropping after divorce, while men's increase. But the deeper pain and shame associated with singleness can tend to keep us quiet.

Since this book is about being real with each other, I'll go ahead and tell you right now that I'm familiar with this territory since I've recently reentered the ranks of single women. Yes, that's hard to admit. I don't enjoy the stigma that comes with being divorced, especially when you're a Christian psychologist and on Christian radio! Yet this is part of who I am, and as much as I'd love to hide it from the world, I'm not going to. My secret is out.

So who are single women? We are Christians and non-Christians. We're never-married, divorced, separated, and widowed. Some are mothers, some desperately *want* to be mothers, and others can take it or leave it. Some are perfectly happy single while others would give anything to enter a different demographic.

The one thing we all have in common is our need to be loved. And for single women, the most common underlying reason for their secret is that they don't feel that basic need is being met. As Gary Chapman puts it, "Married or single, young or old, every human has the emotional need to feel loved. When this need is met, we move out to reach our potential for God and good in the world. However, when we feel unloved, we struggle simply to survive."[2]

If you feel perfectly peaceful and content with your life as it relates to your singlehood, and it's not a cover-up for deeper feelings, then good for you, you may not need this chapter. But for the rest of us, keep reading.

---

## Unlocking the Secret

What are the secrets we keep about our single status?

- We might be secretly glad we don't have to put up with a husband, but we don't talk about it because it just isn't the attitude a good Christian girl should have.
- We may be silent about our desperate desire to be married, not wanting to appear whiny or to be thought of as ungrateful for the gifts God has given us.
- We may be ashamed of being divorced, one of the more frowned-upon sins in the church today.
- We might be keeping quiet about our need to express our sexuality, and we're certainly not telling anyone how we're dealing with that (see chapter 9 for more on this).
- Some of us are desperately afraid of commitment—no wonder, with struggling and failed marriages all around us and tales of abuse more prominent than ever.

+ The desire to have children preoccupies many single
  women, who are mourning the passing of their prime
  childbearing years.

Dayna is a woman in her early forties who's never been married. Every year she sends out a Christmas letter that's a far cry from your average "here's what the kids are doing" update. In fact, her notes read more like a travel brochure. From biking tours of Italy to treks through Machu Picchu, she's been-there-done-that. Dayna shares her thrilling experiences with a positive, upbeat flair, making her married-with-children college buddies (who have hardly traveled farther than the grocery store in years) green with envy at the appearance of her letter each holiday season. Her enthusiasm is real, and her zest for life is a God-given trait that keeps her from wallowing in gloom over what her life is lacking. Yet even Dayna has a secret: she fears her lifelong dream of becoming a wife and mother will never come true. She doesn't talk about it. She's not trying to be fake or put on a facade for the world. She just doesn't feel the need to share this deepest and scariest aspect of herself.

Whether we'd rather be married or we wouldn't, whether we're single by choice or circumstance, whether we long to be mothers or we don't, we're keeping truths about the single experience to ourselves.

## KEEPING THE SECRET

The Christian church is, I think, one of the toughest places to be single. If you're divorced, you feel like a failure and, of course, a sinner. If you've never married, you feel as though people are wondering what's wrong with you. If you're widowed, everyone's feeling sorry for you.

You feel sidelined in singles' groups, railroaded into divorce recovery groups, and exiled from the mainstream life of the church. If you have had a change in marital status through death or divorce, there is a transition period to feeling and seeing yourself as unmarried, and singles' groups only highlight your vulnerable, sudden aloneness. If you've always been single, people assume you have more time to volunteer since you're not tied down with a husband and children. You feel judged if you don't teach Sunday school, run the women's ministry, and head up the community outreach. (After all, what *else* have you got to do?)

It all adds up to not being understood and not feeling valued—and in that atmosphere, why would you share your secrets?

Maybe you want to be married but are afraid of it. Or you were married and are afraid to get hurt again. The commitment is scary, or men have mistreated you enough that you've sworn them off. Or you are single with kids and the dating scene seems too overwhelming or complicated to try. Yet the reality is that most of the women you come in contact with, your friends and acquaintances and book club buddies, are all married. How are you going to share with them the fact that you're afraid of the very situation that defines their lives? You can't. So you stay quiet.

And it's not as though we have many good single-girl role models. The women on *Sex and the City* just don't cut it, at least not if we're trying to live a godly life. The unmarried women in the Bible all seem to be swept up in full-time ministry (or assertively setting man-traps as Ruth did with Boaz), and we may not feel called to that. The life and struggles of a single woman don't seem to be appropriate topics for conversation.

The final hurdle in talking about your experience is that whenever you do, you keep hearing the same old spiritual clichés: *Find your contentment in God alone. Jesus is your husband, and He will meet your needs. You get your value from God, not from other people. Trust God for your future.* While there is deep truth in all of that, these platitudes ignore the real need that you're experiencing. They don't tell you how to deal with desires put there by God in the first place—the desire for a mate, the desire to be loved and touched. They don't tell you how to handle your fears, whether of marriage itself or of never finding someone to marry (or perhaps both). Sharing your secret never seems to get you anywhere, except maybe to feel worse than you already did.

I'm not going to give you platitudes, and I certainly won't minimize your feelings. I'm not going to tell you to shout your truths to the world either. But I am going to help you find some ways to live less painfully with your truth and, hopefully, not experience it as a secret that burdens you any longer.

## Think About It

I've heard sincere Christians say that if we believe we can't be happy without a husband, we are believing a *big lie* perpetuated by the enemy. I wouldn't go this far.

For some women, going through life unmarried is to live in a continual state of near heartbreak. It's a constant reckoning with a dreaded unknown: *Will I stay single the rest of my life? Can this really be true?* I believe these feelings are a reflection of the very deep and real needs God gave us, the need not only to be loved but to give love unconditionally, to share our love sexually, and to create children through a love relationship. You may be keeping secrets because you believe your sadness must mean you're believing the enemy, but I think you're having a realistic response to your situation. You're acknowledging that some of your needs may not, in fact, be met.

This recognition is an extremely important step. If you didn't admit it, you wouldn't be able to do anything to try to address it. While it's beyond the scope of this book for me to give sweeping and detailed advice for how to handle the difficulties inherent in your singlehood, I'd like to offer a few hints to hopefully steer you in the right direction and lift the weight of this secret from your shoulders. At the end of the chapter, I've listed several books that deal honestly with single life, and I'd recommend you take a look at some of them for ways to further ease the stranglehold of your secrets.

*Stop blaming yourself.* The biggest reason we keep our struggles to ourselves is shame, and in being single, our shame is usually involved with the idea that due to our inherent deficits, *we* must be responsible for our singleness. Now, if you're afraid of commitment and consistently sabotage relationships that could lead to marriage, it's important that you own and take responsibility to work through your issues. However, owning your part is different from the self-blaming shame that makes you think, *My being single is a mistake*. If you were married and you were the one who chose divorce, you made some choices that led you here. Figure out why before moving on. Or if your situation is a result of someone else's sin, and you still must bear the burden of dealing with your pain to move forward, see him and his sin for what they are, and don't blame yourself for someone else's failure. Most of the time he didn't leave because you weren't enough but because he didn't have enough inside of him to follow through on his commitment. No matter how much your current situation was caused by your own behavior (and for many of you, it wasn't your behavior at all), hanging on to self-blame will never propel you forward into something better. Blaming yourself keeps you in a victim mode.

Better to acknowledge, "Yes, I did some things that led me here. But that's in the past. I've learned from that, and I'll make better choices from now on." If you need to get into counseling or join a support group in order to learn how to make better choices, then do it. Self-blame is really no better and no more productive than if you were blaming others—it just keeps you stuck. Leaving your past guilt behind and moving forward into a more healthy future is a key to the Christian life. Remember that Paul said in Romans, "There is now no condemnation for those who are in Christ Jesus" (8:1). God does not condemn you, and neither should you condemn yourself.

*Act in the areas of your control.* One of the reasons being single is hard is because we don't have much control over it—either how we got here, or if it will ever end. We don't control whether the perfect guy (unmarried, straight, and without a boatload of baggage) will drop into our lives tomorrow or ever. If he does, we have no control over whether we'll recognize him! We may attempt to control our status through serial dating or joining an Internet matching service, but it's all a gamble. We just don't know.

What we *can* do is identify the areas in which we have some control, and focus there. You absolutely control how you live your life while you're waiting to see what happens next. Let's face it. Complaints are on both sides of the marital fence. So whether married or single, you have other parts of life to tend to that aren't waiting for a status change. You can choose to live as if you're in limbo, trying not to make any big decisions or do anything too exciting, or you can take responsibility for your life and make choices to live the best life you can. I encourage you to make intentional decisions about your life and your time—and live it in the best way you can. Don't hang back with a what-if hanging over your head.

*Get to the root of your fears.* If you've been burned by relationships and are afraid of being involved . . . if you have a fear of commitment as do thousands of women today—fear of losing your independence, being "tied down," having to answer to someone . . . if you're simply afraid of what your life will be like if you never find *the one* . . . you've got to find a way to explore your fears and diffuse them so they can stop defining your life. You can do this through journaling or going to counseling or talking with a trusted friend, and make sure you have at least a single friend or two. But the best way to get out from under the tyranny of fear is to look at it plainly in the light of day, deconstruct it, determine what's realistic about it and what's not, and try to live based on truth rather than fear.

*Remember it's okay to be sad about the loss of a dream.* You may be experiencing ongoing sorrow about being single or not having the family life you thought you would. If you don't get married, you might always experience that sadness to some extent. I don't think it helps to sugarcoat reality, because grief is a part of life. When a beloved parent dies, we may always carry with us a sense of loss and sadness; if we are physically disabled by accident or illness, we'll probably always grieve the loss of our health and mobility. To lose the dream or experience the death of the life you envisioned for yourself is just as painful, and it's important to allow yourself your sorrow.

You are living with an unknown—will you ever be married? It's difficult living with uncertainty, even for short periods of time. Since this is the state of your life right now, allow yourself to experience the emotions that come with it. Seek help from a counselor if the sadness becomes unbearable or changes to ongoing depression and despondency.

*Live life to the fullest.* Like Dayna, who fills her life with friends, a demanding job, active involvement in church activities, and trips to exotic locations, you can choose to live the best life possible regardless of your marital status. Another woman, Avery, is a single mom with a busy life and a full-time job. Yet she finds time to pursue her passion: of all things, rock climbing. For her, it's a uniquely spiritual endeavor. She finds it so challenging and scary that it increases her awareness of God and her reliance on Him; she builds her spiritual and emotional muscles even as she's building her physical ones. Avery has determined to live the fullest life she can, thanking God for her ability to do so.

*Keep hope alive.* Without hope, life ceases to have meaning. As Christians we have the hope of heaven, and to me that says God acknowledges the importance of *hope* to our daily lives. Remember "the hope to which he has called you" (Eph. 1:18) and also remember the hope you still have in this life. What do you hope for? While you're living life to the fullest, do it *expectantly*, never giving up on the hope of your heart's desire.

## SPIRITUAL SECRETS

You may think of your status as a single person as a state of constant suffering to some degree. If so, remember that there can be meaning in suffering, that God can use it not only to shape us but to influence others. Philip Yancey asks how he can find meaning in his suffering, and he wrote:

I begin with the biblical promise that suffering can produce something worthwhile in me. I go through a list
like that in Romans 5, where Paul mentions perseverance,
character, hope, and confidence. "How does suffering
accomplish these?" I ask myself. It produces perseverance,
or steadiness, by slowing me down and forcing me to turn
to God; it produces character by calling on my reserves of
inner strength. I continue through the list, asking how
God can be involved in bringing meaning to the suffering
process.[3]

In my clinical practice, I try to meet people where they are, to
not overspiritualize things, and I never want to minimize people's real
pain. But part of the Christian life does involve going deeper, allowing God to shape us through the difficult experiences in life. We have
to be careful not to "overpsychologize" them either. It takes work, and
it's not pleasant, but we *can* find meaning in our suffering.

Michelle McKinney Hammond is a popular author who has
written several books from her experience as a single woman. In *How
to Avoid the 10 Mistakes Single Women Make*, she discusses the tendency to put marriage on a pedestal next to God. She's learned that
in order to be open to all the blessings God has to offer, we need to
set aside our preconceived notions of what this life was supposed to
be like. We can pray for the grace to be able to let go of what we
expected in order to welcome *what is*.[4]

## From Secrets to Solutions

You may not be able to unload the disappointments involved in
being single, but I believe you can stop carrying the burden of keeping secrets about it.

*Be honest with yourself.* As you're being honest with yourself, try
to discover what secret you might be keeping from yourself about
your single status. Is it fear? Shame? Unworthiness? Self-blame?

*Be honest with God* about your situation. Don't be afraid to cry out to God with your gut-level honesty. Don't be afraid to ask Him why. He can handle everything you've got, and it might be that the only way to find your way through to receiving true comfort from Him is by first being totally real with Him. Remember Hannah, whose story is told in 1 Samuel? Her infertility caused her great pain, and the Scripture says, "In bitterness of soul Hannah wept much and prayed to the Lord" (1:10). God understands bitterness of soul, and He hears you when you weep.

*Be honest with a counselor.* As you've read this chapter, has it occurred to you that you might benefit from talking with a licensed counselor? If so, please don't delay. Are there any friends you can talk to and maybe for the first time be honest about your feelings? Take the risk. Share the burden. Unload your secret.

## PRAYING SCRIPTURE FOR YOUR SECRET

Pray Psalm 25:16–18, 20–21.

Heavenly Father, You know my secrets, and You know how much it hurts me to keep the secrets of being single.

> Turn to me and be gracious to me,
> for I am lonely and afflicted.
> The troubles of my heart have multiplied;
> free me from my anguish.
> Look upon my affliction and my distress
> and take away all my sins . . .
> Guard my life and rescue me;
> let me not be put to shame,
> for I take refuge in you.
> May integrity and uprightness protect me,
> because my hope is in you.

Amen.

## Recommended Resources

*Five Love Languages for Singles,* by Gary Chapman
*How to Avoid the 10 Mistakes Single Women Make* by Michelle
    McKinney Hammond
*How to Get a Date Worth Keeping* by Henry Cloud
*Missing Being Mrs.* by Jennifer Croly
*What to Do Until Love Finds You* by Michelle McKinney
    Hammond
*Where Is God When It Hurts?* by Phillip Yancey

# Chapter 8

# Friendship Isn't Easy

My church, small group, and women's Bible study are not working when it comes to real sharing and making friends. My small group consists of good people, but we are at such different stages in life. I feel like I'm crashing a party when I try to chat with the other women after church.

✦ ✦ ✦

Most of the time, I feel so lonely it hurts. I love being a stay-at-home mom, but I have a lot of trouble making friends with other women.

✦ ✦ ✦

I do not trust people. I'm a good friend to others, but I don't get real and bare myself. In the past when I've done this, I've only been ridiculed and betrayed. You talk about

having safe people to connect with—where do these safe
people live? Not in my world.

Women need strong connections with other women. This is
certainly no secret! The importance of women's friendships
are reflected all around us, in movies and TV shows, in our favorite
novels, in the popularity of book clubs and spa days and coffee dates,
even in the church's fervent attempts to build their women's ministries. From *Thelma and Louise*, to Monica and Rachel on *Friends*, to
the women on *Desperate Housewives*, to Jane Austen's popular hero-
ines, portrayals of female friendships permeate the culture, for better
and worse.

For all of history, women have gathered together and relied on
one another for support, conversation, and laughter. In everything
from giving birth to borrowing a cup of sugar to shopping and baby
showers, the rituals of girlfriends give shape and substance to our
lives. It's an aspect of life that can't be replaced by husbands or boyfriends or children or parents. And while some might beg to disagree,
it's a part of life that is not meant to be replaced by God either.

In fact, the idea of friendship is such an integral part of life that
we naturally expect it to be effortless, instinctive. That's where the
difficulty comes from—and that is where our secrets lie. It's a star-
tling discovery to find that friendship, rather than being the answer
to our problems, can instead be the cause.

---

## UNLOCKING THE SECRET

We all need connections to other people. In fact, one of the most
common underlying issues for clients who come to my office is a
lack of appropriate connection with others, whether it's their parents,
their spouses, their kids, or their friends. Solid and deep same-sex
friendships are one of the most important necessities on our way to
increasing our emotional maturity as adults. Yet our culture seems to

have reached an all-time low in terms of our ability to make and maintain these connections.

We're all just so busy these days, aren't we? Between our jobs and our families and our church activities and maybe some Little League thrown in, who has time for friends? The busyness that *fills* our time also robs us of the time for friends. It's no wonder "virtual friendship" has become normal for people of all ages. Facebook and MySpace and the blogosphere are taking the place of real-live, let's-get-together-for-coffee connections. And it's taking a toll on all of us.

The secrets women are carrying about friendship tend to fall into two general categories. The first is a lack of fulfilling female friendships, and the biggest reason for this is our lack of time to nurture and invest in relationships with other women. I see this in all ages and types of women. Those with families and jobs are always strapped for time. Older women (empty nesters and retirees) may have too much time but not enough friendships to fill it. If they were too busy in their younger years to gather a group of long-standing friends, it's very difficult to do it at this stage. Younger women who don't have husbands or kids often have many friends but no deeply significant relationships.

The second type of secret women keep about friendship is how intense female relationships can be and the depth of the pain we feel when they go wrong. Betrayal, competition, and backbiting among women can cause rifts as devastating as the breakup of a long-standing love relationship, including marriage. This intensity with female friendships starts way back in preschool and reaches a height in the elementary and preteen years. This may be because our female friendships are the precursors to our later love relationships. We care first what our girlfriends think of us before we are ever interested in boys. Even as adult women, we check with each other about what to wear to make sure we'll fit in with the other women.

In their attempts to manage relationships, girls begin early using social aggression and exclusion to deal with acceptance/rejection issues, hurt, betrayal, and the need to know they are liked. Marion

K. Underwood, in her book *Social Aggression Among Girls*, wrote about the dilemma girls have. In our culture, girls receive conflicting messages about dealing with negative emotions: we are encouraged to be honest with our feelings, but if you want people to like you, you must refrain and be "everything nice."[1] One woman wrote in with this observation:

> My secret is that I feel alienated from other women. I believe this comes from being abandoned by my mother and criticized by my older sister. Deep inside I need women to affirm me. I believe women live in fear of being rejected or judged by other women. Society tells us we are of less value than men, so in an attempt to feel better about ourselves, we compete with each other. I really just want to be friends with women.

This woman is reflecting a very real need we all have. *We just want to be friends.*

## KEEPING THE SECRET

So why is this such a deep, dark, hidden aspect of being a woman? Why are we burdened with the "secrets" of our friend troubles?

Michelle is an outgoing woman in her forties, married with two children. When her kids were babies, she developed friendships with a group of six other at-home moms, two of whom became her close friends. She was used to having this group of women available, whether to chat on the phone, to go out for a girls' night, or to meet at the park during the day with the kids. But then Michelle and her family relocated several states away, leaving behind her friends. Making things more difficult, she went to work full time, so the community of at-home moms was no longer available to her. She was lonely but kept telling herself to give it time, that she'd find friends. Now, five years later, Michelle has a wide circle of local acquaintances, several long-distance best friends, and an active social life . . . as a blogger. While she yearns for girlfriends with whom she can go shopping or meet for a spontaneous lunch, she settles for cell phone calls while carpooling and lots of cyber-communication at the laptop. Whenever she has time to stop and think about it—which isn't often—Michelle admits to herself that she is undeniably lonely.

I love the old childhood song: "Make new friends, but keep the old; some are silver, and the other gold!" There are different seasons of life, and change is inevitable. We have to learn how to navigate those changes. Some friends we will keep for a lifetime, but at different times they will take on a greater or lesser prominence in our lives. We have to be open to adding new people if only for a season of life, as some will come and go. If you think you've already made all of the friends you'll ever need or want, think again—you might be left behind as people's lives change.

Old friends are sometimes safe and secure, because we have history with them and they already know us and hopefully like us. The downside is that we can sometimes stay stuck in the past with them, and they can't always see the person we've become since way back when. Newer friends meet us at our more mature state or accept us as the professional, capable adults we are. The disadvantage is that they may be more transient and attached to a job, community, or activity, and when any of those ends, it is more effort to stay in contact. Therefore we need a balance of a few old friends who have known us over time and some new ones who keep us active and moving forward.

The irony of the secrets women keep about friendship is this: if we had satisfying and fulfilling friendships, we wouldn't have the secret. If we had someone with whom to share our secret, we wouldn't have the secret in the first place, right? We keep the secret of our lack of friendship because, well, we don't have the right friends to share it with.

There are other reasons we don't talk about our loneliness. We believe the myth that if we're married, we're supposed to be satisfied with the husband-wife connection. We're not supposed to *need* anyone else because, after all, our husbands are supposed to be our best friends, right? But the truth is, whether or not you think of your spouse as your BFF (and I'm not going to weigh in on that one), you still need to bond with other women.

Another myth that keeps our friend issues a secret is that we're supposed to have Jesus as our best friend. Undoubtedly this is true—but Jesus never intended for you to rely on Him to the exclusion of other humans. God gave each of us the deep need and desire to connect with others on many levels. Friendship is one of our needs if we're to have wholeness and grow spiritually and emotionally.

Sometimes we're afraid to admit our loneliness and lack of friends because we believe we're the only one feeling this way. It seems as if everyone else has friends, and we're the only ones feeling disconnected. Clearly this isn't true. Loneliness and lack of a close circle of friends are some of the things we talk about with callers quite frequently on *New Life Live!* And many women wrote to us about how painful these issues are for them.

Finally, friendships tap into the deepest part of us, affecting our self-worth. If we're rejected or betrayed by a friend, we can interpret it to mean there's something wrong with us. We believe there must be something unlikable or unworthy about us, and we may begin to feel ashamed of who we are. With those kinds of feelings, we're certainly not in a place where we want to admit it to others. So we keep secrets about our friendship troubles.

## THINK ABOUT IT

I may not be able to help you solve all of your friendship problems. But I want to share a few things that might help you see how important our friends really are, why it's normal to feel lonely if we don't have the right connections in our lives, and some of the ways we can increase our chances of having fulfilling relationships with other women. Here are some friendship issues that tend to give us the most trouble.

*I don't know how to make friends.* Thinking back to early childhood, I don't remember feeling that it was an effort to make friends. It seemed as though whoever was around was just automatically my "friend," someone to join me on the swings and slide, someone with whom to play jacks or hide-and-seek. It was somewhere around middle school that friendship seemed to become an effort, and as I got older, the idea of making friends became less natural, more intentional, and more fraught with possible hazards.

Think back to your childhood. At what point did it seem to become more difficult to have and maintain friends? How did you handle it? You may be surprised to realize that today as an adult, you're still handling your friendship troubles the same way you did when you were thirteen. Part of growing into maturity as an adult is letting go of those old patterns and creating new ones. Maybe you never really learned the art of making friends, but it's not too late.

The most important factor to remember is these four words: *it's not about you.* That's right. When you focus on others—understanding who they are, communicating that you care—you take the pressure off yourself. You don't have to act a certain way, and you don't have to gain others' approval, because it's not about you. Developing the art of friendship can be a long, ongoing process, but the single best way to get started is to start showing genuine interest in other people.

You might have a multitude of acquaintances, but you're wishing for deeper friendships. Begin to demonstrate deeper caring about some of these women. Ask them how they are. Follow up on any concerns they share with you by phoning or e-mailing for an update. I know it sounds simple. And it's not the last word on friendship. But it can be the first step beyond "I don't know how to make friends" and toward a small circle of relationships that count.

*I've been burned by friends, and I don't want to go through that again.* Like the woman who wrote to the New Life Secrets Blog, wondering where all the "safe people" are, you may have good reasons to be gun-shy about making new friends. This is a tough one, because like most things in life, it involves a balance. We need to be cautious about whom we choose to trust; yet we need to take risks sometimes and reach out to others, or we'll never have any friends.

If you've experienced painful betrayal and rejection, I suggest you acknowledge this honestly to yourself, commit to taking those lessons with you into the future, and move slowly back into attempting to make friends. Be willing to look honestly at any patterns or themes in yourself that keep recurring in your friendships. As is true in dating relationships, the healthier you are, the more you will attract the right people for you.

Lasting friendships happen slowly and incrementally over time. If you are scared to jump in again or don't trust others or your choices, a safe way to start is to get involved in a ministry, volunteer work, or an activity you like. Anything of interest to you that you might choose for the activity itself could work. The key is that it has repeated exposure to others in your age and stage of life. This gives you opportunity to be alongside others in a safe way and be able to get to know them in a context. Initially, you may not think anyone is friendship material, but over time, as familiarity grows, you may be surprised at what develops. Some of my best friends have been people I had no initial interest in, but I grew to see their quality over time. While instant fast friends are exciting and new, just as with infatuation, they don't always stand the test of time, and then once again we are hurt.

Remember that your experience doesn't represent what *all* people are like, and many others are hurting just like you. You'll need to take steps to heal from your previous unhappy relationship so you can move on to more healthy ones in the future. Please don't buy into lies like "It's just not worth it" or "It's impossible to make good friends these days." Your past rejection doesn't have to define your future.

*I'm afraid they won't like me.* Many of us have self-worth issues going all the way back to childhood. When we feel as though we never measure up, then of course we won't be enthusiastic about trying to make friends. This is why it's important to do the emotional and psychological work of learning to accept both ourselves and others for who they are. Once we stop expecting perfection from ourselves and learn to be comfortable with who we are (warts and all), it becomes so much easier to open up to genuine friendship.

Of course, it's easy to get stuck in a sort of time warp. Your adult self knows intellectually that you have worth and that God loves and accepts you. But emotionally you may have "pockets" of vulnerability in which you're still four years old (or ten or sixteen), needing the approval from those around you, looking for what you didn't get when you should have, such as unconditional acceptance from your parents. It's easy for you to interpret the actions of others in light of your own worth.

For example, if you don't get invited to a party, it may tap into a time when you were seven years old and your next-door neighbor excluded you from her birthday celebration. You may feel this episode simply confirms what you already knew—that you're really not okay, not likable, not acceptable. You'll know you've made progress when you can experience a disappointment from a friend and not automatically assume it means something negative about you. Instead, you'll think something along the lines of, *Hmmm, I really thought we were friends. I wonder why she did this? I guess I was wrong about my importance to her. Maybe someday I'll find out what went wrong.* The bottom line is that if you're always shying away from making friends because of your fear that they won't like you, this is a sign to do two things: explore why you're still stymied by these residues from your past, and as I just mentioned, begin to focus more on the other person instead of yourself.

*I don't have time to nurture friendships.* Many women are pulled in twenty different directions, and if they had any extra time, they'd probably opt for a good nap . . . or perhaps a manicure—alone. If this is where you are, please believe me, I know exactly what it's like. I'm a single mother with a burgeoning psychology practice that entails private clients, counseling people on the radio at *New Life Live!* and, obviously, writing. I have all the usual church commitments, and my children have their own activities that keep me running. "I don't have time" has become the story of my life.

I don't want you to think I'm trying to say I'm doing everything right because I'm not. But I have to say that female friendships have become all the more important to me as my life has gotten busier. Without them, I don't think I would have made it through the last few years of the turmoil of divorce, and I don't think I'd be keeping my sanity today. My girlfriends help keep me centered, they give me reality checks, they make me laugh, and they keep me from being lonely.

It doesn't take much. Grabbing coffee between appointments, chatting on cell phones between activities, giving each other e-mail updates and atta-girls and you-can-do-its. In fact, I look at my friendships as necessary if I'm going to keep all the other balls in the air.

Don't have time? Please rethink this one. Ask a girlfriend to meet you for lunch or catch a movie or come to your house while the kids play. If you don't have girlfriends, ask an acquaintance—maybe she'll become your girlfriend. Afraid everyone else will say no because they're too busy? Be persistent. In my mind, we can't let that tyrannical boss "time" steal our opportunities for one of the most joyful and necessary parts of life. We need friends. Don't use the time excuse. Make it happen.

*I'm doing all the right things, but it's not working. I'm still lonely.* It can be so frustrating to feel like the writer of the very first paragraph in this chapter, who said, "My church, small group, and Bible study are not working when it comes to making friends." Are you in this situation? Maybe you're in a book club, moms group, or Bible study. Perhaps you participate in PTA and serve in ministry and try to stay active, but you're still lonely.

My friend Justine used to feel this way too. She was always involved in activities with other women but felt lonely and wondered why the groups she was in weren't working. One day she got into an extended conversation with one of the other moms at her kids' school, and she was shocked when the woman referred to the fact that Justine was "always so perfect" and that the other moms weren't sure how to approach her. That wasn't at all how Justine had seen herself, and it prompted her to make a serious examination of her behavior when in these groups of women.

Sure enough, Justine realized her own insecurities had made her do a few things guaranteed to scare other women away: She always tried to dress nicely and look her best even if only dropping her kids off at sports; she was quiet and rarely initiated a conversation (which others interpreted as standoffish); and when people did talk to her, she didn't make efforts to prolong the conversation. Justine's self-examination led to a profound change in the way she related to the women around her. She began showing more interest in them, asking them questions, and intentionally trying to get to know them. She tried to relax and not worry so much about what they thought of her, realizing they were more concerned about what *she* thought of *them*. She figured out that to make friends, she was going to have to go the extra mile: invite someone to her home for tea or drop by someone's house with a book the two of them could discuss. Justine realized that she'd *thought* she was doing all the right things, but in reality she wasn't. With persistence, it wasn't long before she had a couple of new friends, and she knew they were the real deal. But it wouldn't have happened without an honest evaluation of her behavior and a commitment to doing things differently.

Friends are crucial to sustaining our emotional life. As Jeff Wickwire said in his book *Friendships*, "Friendships are absolutely relevant in our walk with God. We are hardwired to relate to others. God has placed a 'friend-shaped' hole in every soul."[2] This is where we can share our secrets—all the things we're talking about in this book—and where we can learn we are acceptable, even with our secrets. Don't underestimate the importance of learning to *be* a good friend in order to *have* good friends.

## SPIRITUAL SECRETS

It's not just in the realm of psychology that we've discovered the importance of friendship. The Bible gives us numerous examples of enduring friendships: David and Jonathan, Naomi and Ruth, Mary and Elizabeth, Paul and Timothy. Jesus gave high importance to it, expressing to His disciples how important they were to Him as friends. He showed us a good model of how friendship works, too, with His close inner circle (Peter, James, and John), His slightly larger outer circle (the rest of the disciples and others, like Mary, Martha, and Lazarus), and the rest of His followers, who weren't really close friends but valued acquaintances.

One of my favorite verses is from Ecclesiastes: "If one falls down, his friend can help him up. But pity the man who falls and has no one to help him up!" (4:10). We need our friends to help us when we fall, as well as to celebrate with us when things are going well.

So how can our faith help us in our approach to making and keeping friends? We can acknowledge that God has provided us with the desire for friendship because He wants us to live out our lives in positive, affirming relationships with one another. We can follow the example of Jesus, investing ourselves in others and building lasting bonds. We can see potential friends as gifts from God and decide to accept the gift.

C. S. Lewis wrote, "Friendship is unnecessary, like philosophy, like art, like the universe itself (for God did not need to create). It has no survival value; rather, it is one of those things which give value to survival."[3] Let's not underestimate the value of friends in our lives. Let's not push them away because friendships are difficult or because making friends doesn't seem the best use of our time. Let's overcome our fears and seek to make authentic, lasting friendships an integral part of our lives.

## FROM SECRETS TO SOLUTIONS

The secrets we keep about the difficulty of finding and keeping friends are painful—not just because we don't *want* to share them, but because we might not have anyone we feel comfortable sharing them with. So how can we free ourselves from the burdens of these secrets?

As you become honest with yourself about your difficulties with friendship, you might uncover some fears, some hesitancy based on past hurts, or some insecurities. You might realize you've devalued the idea of friendship, thinking it wasn't a very "spiritual" pursuit. Or you may be like my friend Justine and realize you simply haven't been acting like someone who wants friends. Whatever you discover, I urge you to take steps to deal honestly with that reality.

Don't be afraid to be honest with God about your desire for friends. But please don't be like so many women I know who pray and beg God to send friends, and then sit back and wait for likely prospects to cross their path. Pray for friends—then pray for the wisdom to know when to step out of your comfort zone and open your heart to a possible friend, and the courage to *do it*. This is not one of those "sit back and wait for God to work" situations. I believe God wants to bring you friends—but He'll do it by showing you how to *be* a friend.

If your fears about friendships run deep, talk with a counselor about it. You would be amazed at the steps forward you can take once you have some help and gain some insight. With the courage and conviction to make new friends, a whole new world could open up to you.

Tracy Klehn wrote, "So then, what is our responsibility with regard to friendship? *I believe that we have the choice to connect with the beauty that God places in our lives.* We have the choice to *receive* the gift of friendship and to *invite others* to do the same by extending our hearts to them."[4] That is my prayer for you, that you would receive the gift and offer it to others as well.

## Praying Scripture for Your Secret

Pray John 15:12–17.

Jesus, You said, "Love each other as I have loved you." Help me, Lord, to love others as You have loved me. "Greater love has no one than this, that she lay down her life for her friends." Teach me to do this in a healthy and appropriate way. Thank You for choosing me. Help me to remain in You and remain in Your love, and teach me to love others as You have commanded. Thank You for Your precious love, Lord Jesus. Amen.

## Recommended Resources

*Come Rain or Come Shine: Friendships Between Women* by Linda Bucklin and Mary Keil

*Friendships: Avoiding the Ones that Hurt, Finding the Ones that Heal* by Jeff Wickwire

*Growing Friendships: Connecting More Deeply with Those Who Matter Most* by Tracy Klehn

*Grown Up Girlfriends* by Erin Smalley and Carrie Oliver

*The Four Loves* by C. S. Lewis

*The Friendships of Women* by Dee Brestin

# Part Three

## SECRETS ABOUT SEXUALITY

—

# Chapter 9

# My Husband and I Have Different Sexual Needs

I love my husband, but I hate having sex. Sometimes I find myself repulsed by the thought of having sex. It is such a chore. And I cannot stand kissing him. I feel ashamed to admit this. I don't think I'm sexually attracted to my husband. Is that possible even though I still love him?

◆ ◆ ◆

When women get together, and someone inevitably makes a little joke about how her husband always wants sex, and everyone giggles and rolls their eyes and complains and whines about what pigs men are, I just want to scream and shake them. The great American joke is all about how the wife has a headache, and the husband always has to beg for sex. Apparently, I am the only woman in the world who had to beg her husband for sex and was always refused. Nobody talks about that humiliating secret.

Leeann and Michelle were friends in their thirties, each married with two young children. As their friendship grew closer, Leeann began to reveal some dissatisfaction in her marriage—namely, that her husband wanted sex every day. With a six-month-old baby and a two-year-old, Leeann was so exhausted she'd completely lost interest. Sometimes she "gave in," and other times she refused. She and her husband were always angry with each other, and her marriage was becoming increasingly unpleasant.

As Leeann shared her growing frustration, Michelle tried to offer encouragement and advice but was at a loss for anything truly helpful to say. The one thing she didn't do was commiserate from a perspective of "having been there," and Leeann began to notice. She finally questioned Michelle: "Why don't you tell me how it is for *you*? You always give me advice, but you never talk about your situation. I feel like I'm telling you all my secrets, but you're not telling me yours. What's going on?"

Michelle was embarrassed but finally had to open up. She couldn't relate to Leeann's situation because hers was the opposite: her husband never wanted sex. Michelle was always the one initiating things, and even then, her husband sometimes said no. "I'm too tired," was his standard response.

Michelle and Leeann couldn't believe how different their marriages were but realized the result was the same. They were both becoming unhappy and disconnected in their marriages. They loved their husbands, and they felt their husbands loved them . . . but why was each couple so massively out of sync?

---

## Unlocking the Secret

Most of us who've been married for any length of time can relate to this secret in one way or another. The sexual aspect of a marriage plays a huge role in our lives—how we feel about ourselves and how we see our spouses—but it's obviously very personal, so it's not surprising that many women keep it a secret.

Numerous women wrote to say that they don't enjoy sex with their husbands or have experienced a long-term lack of desire.

> My secret is not much of a secret. Anyone who knows me at all, including my husband, knows that I do not enjoy sex. The guilt and pressure I feel is enormous, and I wish it would just go away.

✦ ✦ ✦

> I wish my husband had *no* sex drive. Sex makes my stomach turn.

These women seem to fit into our culture's (incorrect) stereotype that men "want it all the time" and women only tolerate sex. It's more socially acceptable when your intimate issues are along these lines—after all, most people aren't surprised when a woman says that her husband wants more bedroom action than she does.

But by far the most letters I received were about the opposite problem, a hugely underreported reality in marriages.

> I desire sex more than my husband, and this disappoints me immensely. I feel hurt and fooled by the stereotypes given in most marriage books which assume higher male desire and encourage the woman to initiate, be available, and see sex as spiritual. (I already do.) I am confused and deeply saddened. Where is the acknowledgment of this male/female "reversal" of desire? Refusing to write about women who desire sex more than their husbands only makes women and men in this situation feel ashamed and inadequate.

✦ ✦ ✦

My secret is that for twenty-four years my husband has not wanted to make love, yet he continues to be a devoted father and life partner. I feel that an entire part of my life has been ignored, dishonored, and devalued. I have addressed it with him, but he refuses to discuss it. I have shown anger, patience, and forgiveness. I have attempted to change my thoughts, feelings, and beliefs. How do I let this go and move on in my feelings about myself, our relationship, and our life?

*   *   *

My husband doesn't want intimacy. How do I excite him again?

Michele Weiner-Davis, author of *The Sex-Starved Wife*, goes so far as to say, "I'm convinced that low sexual desire in men is America's best-kept secret."[1] (It should tell you something that there is even a book with that title!) In a culture obsessed with sex, it's definitely surprising that so many people—both women and men—would rather opt out.

## Keeping the Secret

So if this discrepancy of desire in marriage is so common, why is it such a big secret? It goes beyond the fact that our intimate life within marriage is something normally kept private. Our sex lives cut to the very heart of our perception of ourselves as normal. When we don't feel normal, we are unlikely to share it with anyone.

The secrets about our marital sex lives weigh on us because we think we are unusual. We think we are the only couple who struggles in this area. If you're a wife with more desire than your husband, you're probably suffering deep assaults on your sense of being desirable, feminine, sexy, or even lovable. When your husband doesn't desire you physically, you interpret it as a rejection of your very being. It seems so basic—all men are hot for it all the time, right? You wonder what is so wrong with *you* that your husband couldn't care less.

If you're in the opposite camp, completely disinterested in sex, you're probably awash with guilt. You have a strong feeling you *should* desire to please your husband. You wish you could take pleasure and receive love this way. You want that aspect of your life to be exciting. But you simply have no interest—or even more than that, you are actively repulsed by the thought of physical intimacy. The women's magazines make it clear that you're supposed to be hot for your guy. So you are full of shame on top of the guilt. You constantly wonder, *What's wrong with me?*

The embarrassment, guilt, humiliation, feelings of inadequacy, feelings of being unusual—all these keep us carrying the secret.

## Think About It

When husbands and wives experience a long-term discrepancy in their interest in sex, they're often tempted to minimize it and rationalize it. "After all, it's just sex." But nothing could be further from the truth. Spouses are meant to connect with each other physically through intimate touch and loving expressions of their sexuality. Of course, there are times in every marriage when a couple is unable to relate this way, and as long as it doesn't continue indefinitely, it's not a problem. But frequently I see people who have developed a pattern in their marriage whereby one partner is always the seducer, and the other is always disinterested, and this affects every aspect of the relationship. The sexual arena can be a snapshot of the marital dynamics.

In *The Sex-Starved Wife*, author Davis wrote, "It's not just about sex. It's about feeling wanted, loved, appreciated, sexy, and attractive. It's about feeling close and connected. Sex is truly the tie that binds; it leads to emotional intimacy. And when the spouse with a lower sex drive doesn't understand this, it spells trouble for the marriage."[2]

I believe the converse is also true for women: emotional intimacy leads to the desire for sexual closeness. Women tend to have sex with their minds first and their bodies second.

I know that if you've found yourself either wanting more intimacy than your husband or not wanting any physical involvement at all, you're probably surprised. You never thought you'd find yourself in this situation! Dr. Linda Mintle, in her book *Divorce-Proofing Your Marriage*, discusses how emotional and sexual distance, left unattended, can slowly erode a relationship as the gap widens over time, setting unsuspecting couples up for divorce twenty years down the road. The level of intimacy, both emotional and sexual, is a barometer for the health of a marital relationship.[3] Therefore, awareness and attention are key in every marriage.

Sometimes the more we know a person, the more critical we are of his or her shortcomings and the less safe we feel about being vulnerable. If you have fears about being truly intimate with another human being (everyone does to a certain degree) or fears related to distance and closeness or fears of being abandoned, controlled, or engulfed, this can make sexual intimacy more difficult. In our most significant relationships, wonderful healing and interconnectedness can be cultivated, especially in the context of a loving marital commitment. However, within this same relationship, we can regress to our most primitive selves and act out all of our unresolved hurts in which the bedroom becomes the stage for this psychological, sexual, emotional play to unravel.

Take comfort in the fact that you are *not* unusual, and you're definitely not alone. We live in a world that has an extremely disordered view of sexuality. Pornography and sex outside of marriage have become normalized, and erotic images are available everywhere you look. It's only natural that our culture's warped sexual identity affects individuals and marriages. But that doesn't mean you are fated to remain in your unhappy situation. I want you to begin thinking about letting go of the shame and the self-blame, and begin to adopt a proactive attitude of truly wanting to improve this area of your life.

You may be one of the women who wrote me, disappointed and disillusioned that there doesn't seem to be a good selection of resources addressing your secret. But that just isn't true anymore. As you'll see from the list at the end of this chapter, numerous books are now addressing both sides of this issue and offering valuable advice. In this brief format, I obviously can't give you all the answers. But I want to point you in the right direction so that you have three things firmly in your mind: (1) that your sex life in marriage is important, (2) that your situation is not unusual but is a reality for many in our sex-saturated culture, and (3) that help is available through books, through counseling, through prayer and reliance on God, and through determining to change the way you're approaching and thinking about things.

Psychologists have long known that a healthy sex life within marriage is an important contributor to overall health—physical as well as emotional. Today there are also more medical doctors specializing in sexual medicine to help both men and women with physical, hormonal, or neurochemical issues that become obstacles to the enjoyment and function of healthy sexual activity. And as stated earlier, a disconnect in the physical aspect of marriage is usually a symptom of other issues in the relationship; and this disconnect can cause or worsen any issues that are already there. As Gary Chapman wrote in *The Five Love Languages*, physical touch is "a powerful vehicle for communicating marital love. Holding hands, kissing, embracing, and sexual intercourse are all ways of communicating emotional love to one's spouse."[4] Without this healthy means of expression, the relationship can quickly go downhill.

*If you are the spouse who is disinterested in sex:* First, it's important to acknowledge that you might have some powerful reasons for feeling this way. Have you explored this in therapy with a professional? Some common explanations for lack of desire are negative sexual experiences or molestation in your past, resentment or anger toward your husband (which can relate to a whole multitude of issues), not being physically attracted to your husband, lack of trust, fear of vulnerability, and emotional disconnect. Don't rule out a physical issue such as a hormonal imbalance. It's easy to simply think, *That's just the way I am*, and refuse to explore it any further. But remember our feelings come and go, and nothing will ever change with that perspective.

Look beyond the obvious problem. How is the communication in your marriage? Do you trust your husband to handle your vulnerability with care? Is your husband a disappointment to you in some way? Is he not living up to your expectations? Or maybe this has to do with something in your past. Whatever it is, it's vital that you uncover it and stop carrying the burden of this secret alone.

If you have a persistent lack of sex drive or even disgust toward sex, you're probably not excited or motivated to begin exploring this area of your life. But healthy sexual relating with your spouse is a really good thing—worth getting right. This is why the *secret* aspect of this has got to go: you can begin processing this in the *right* way with the *right* person so things can change.

One thing I hear quite often from women who don't desire a physical connection with their husbands is that they are ashamed of their own bodies. Perhaps you've gained weight; maybe you don't look anything like a supermodel or our culture's "ideal" image of a sexy woman. Let me tell you something: none of us fits that image! Many husbands know that they are not Prince Charming either, and your husband probably doesn't see you as you see yourself. Ask your husband if he would rather be physically close with you as you are or wait until you get that perfect body back. If your husband is the one with the problem regarding your body, then that is a different issue—his, not yours—but tell yourself honestly whose critical voice you're hearing in your head. Your path is twofold: take steps to begin learning how to accept yourself as a lovingly made child of God, and also take steps to increase your feeling of physical health and well-being.

I understand these things are easy to say but hard to do. They will require effort on your part, and they'll require giving up your secret, getting it out in the open—at least in your own mind—so that you can deal with it. But it's crucial to face the underlying self-image concerns if you want to get out from under the secret of your unhappy sex life (more about self-image in part 5).

*If your husband is the one with the low sex drive:* You have grown up with the idea permeating our culture that all men want sex all the time. So when your husband seemed to be lacking interest, you were probably confused. Your first thought was likely, *What's wrong with me?* As time went on, your feelings have probably intensified into feeling totally undesirable, and you may now be angry or resentful toward your husband.

Mary was in this situation. For several years, her husband was always "too tired." She continually wondered about it, thinking he must have stopped seeing her as sexy once she'd given birth to two children. Sometimes she'd wonder if maybe he was having an affair. Or could he even be gay? But there were no other signs that these suspicions could be true (although unfortunately, for some women they are). So Mary figured her husband must have a physical problem and repeatedly asked him to see a doctor. He never did, and nothing ever changed. Eventually, when her kids were a little older, she went back to working full time outside the home. It didn't take long for her to discover that there was no shortage of men who were attracted to her. She became involved in numerous flirtations and was propositioned more than once. Now she began to look at her husband with disdain, thinking, *How did I marry the one guy on earth who doesn't want to have sex with me?* The situation grew worse, and her resentment and blame toward her husband increased until she nearly succumbed to an affair.

At this point Mary realized things were out of control. She told her husband what was going on and insisted they get counseling and begin to address the disconnect between them. She didn't offer an ultimatum but simply told the truth: "These last few years of being physically neglected by you have left me feeling completely worthless. I've discovered that I am a desirable person after all—so I'm no longer willing to accept the status quo. Please help me work on our marriage so that we'll both feel loved, appreciated, and excited to be together."

Mary's story has a happy ending, but it only came after a great deal of effort. In fact, things got worse before they got better, and Mary and her husband came perilously close to divorce. That was four years ago, and now they have a stronger marriage and a rejuvenated sex life. Mary and her husband both acknowledge that their commitment to making things work in the bedroom works wonders for all the other aspects of their relationship.

I know that not every story ends perfectly. Not all couples are able to come back together in the spirit of rebuilding a strong marriage. But there is *no chance* of improvement if you don't at least try. I encourage you to stop suffering alone with your secret, and begin considering ways to improve your situation.

## Spiritual Secrets

If you are a wife suffering with a sexual discrepancy in your marriage, you might wonder what good it will do for you to be reading this. After all, it's a problem with the two of you, right? It's not just about you. Be assured that even if your husband chooses not to cooperate with you in trying to find some sexual common ground, you are not doomed. God can work in *your* heart and mind, regardless of what anyone else is doing. He can change your response to your situation, He can bring ideas and wisdom to your mind, and He can even work so powerfully through you that your husband can't help but change. Trust God for this.

As individuals we always have the power to act, whether or not anyone else joins us in that action. We can choose to either change our situation or change our response to an unchangeable situation. This means you can make the decision to stop keeping this secret and instead *act* to try and make it better.

Scripture encourages us to speak the truth in love. John says,

"Let us not love with words or tongue but with actions and in truth" (1 John 3:18). We can honor our husbands by speaking the truth to them—lovingly.

I once listened to a radio program in which a woman called in complaining about her husband's lack of sex drive. She said she'd tried talking to him about it, but every time, they "just ended up in a huge fight." There could be exceptions to this, but I honestly can't see how the conversation would end in a fight if the truth were being spoken with genuine love, compassion, and understanding.

Many women wrote to our Secrets Blog, saying, "I've tried everything." I challenge you to ask yourself whether you've done everything possible. Have you spoken the truth—with love? And if so, would your husband report feeling loved by your conversation with him?

If you have, you now need to try something *different*. Most people say they've tried everything without realizing they've actually tried the one or two things they could think of to do, over and over again. Doing the same thing repeatedly is not going to get different results. Time to find a new approach.

Trust that God's intent is for you to have a loving physical and emotional relationship with your husband. Pray for it, act on it, and keep acting on it. Don't give up.

## From Secrets to Solutions

Carrying around this secret is not doing you any good, as you already know. Your marriage doesn't stand still—it's always changing, either for better or for worse. If you have a problem and you're not addressing it, then chances are your marriage is deteriorating before your eyes. Your goal right now is to diffuse the secret, to strip it of its power to weigh you down, and get your marriage moving in the right direction.

*Be honest with yourself.* Now is the time to get real with the hold this secret has over you. Begin to explore it and ask yourself how and why the situation got to be what it is. Tell yourself some truths:

- I am not abnormal or unusual. This situation is common but usually hidden.
- I am not doomed to live this way forever.
- I can choose to act in the areas in which I have power—by working on myself, my attitude, and my choices.
- It's not okay to live in a sexless marriage unless *both* partners have agreed out loud that these are the terms of their relationship (not just through silent resignation).
- There is help for me. I just need to find it.

*Be honest with God.* Pray about your secret. Ask God to reveal to you anything you're not seeing clearly. Search your heart, and confess if you find resentment and anger, resignation, self-pity. Tell God you are ready to find a new way to approach your marriage, and ask Him to guide you and give you courage.

*Be honest with your husband.* This is one of those situations in which your secret is not yours alone—it belongs to your partner too. You may have already told him about it countless times, too many times, and he's sick of hearing it. This time, talk with him differently. Think about who your husband is and how he best receives information. Talk honestly from your heart but without emotional drama or histrionics. Use only *I* statements instead of *you* statements. Think about how Mary approached her husband. She was no longer looking for him to make her okay. She didn't put him down but told him lovingly what she was and wasn't willing to live with. She took herself more seriously and was clear about what she wanted for them both. Let him hear that your goal is to love him better, that it's about both of you having a more satisfying marriage. Talk to him about your ideas for getting help in this area. Ask him if he is willing to join you in these efforts. Ask him about his thoughts or ideas. Then be specific with what you are asking each of you to do once you have agreed on a plan. Be aware that this doesn't always happen in the first conversation. He (or you) may need time and space to consider what you each are truly willing to do.

If you've talked to him about it in the past with only negative results, it may take some time for him to hear you. It may take some strategizing on your part to find different ways to approach him so that he knows you are not being critical of him. Remember, say everything with love. And if you've found anger and resentment getting in the way, you'll need to address it before you can be successful having this conversation with your husband.

*Be honest with a therapist or counseling professional.* As you know, problems in the bedroom usually mean larger issues are present in the relationship. If your husband agrees, seek marriage counseling to begin identifying the issues that are coming between you. If he's not interested, you'll benefit from some counseling on your own. Your goal is to come to a better, healthier place in your own heart and mind and, hopefully, to put together a game plan for ramping up the intimate part of your marriage.

## PRAYING SCRIPTURE FOR YOUR SECRET

Pray 1 Corinthians 7:2–5 (MSG):

> It's good for a man to have a wife, and for a woman to have a husband. Sexual drives are strong, but marriage is strong enough to contain them and provide for a balanced and fulfilling sexual life in a world of sexual disorder. The marriage bed must be a place of mutuality—the husband seeking to satisfy his wife, the wife seeking to satisfy her husband. Marriage is not a place to "stand up for your rights." Marriage is a decision to serve the other, whether in bed or out. Abstaining from sex is permissible for a period of time if you both agree to it, and if it's for the purposes of prayer and fasting—but only for such times.

Then come back together again. Satan has an ingenious way of tempting us when we least expect it.

Lord, help us to make Your view of marriage a reality in our lives. Teach us to satisfy one another not only in the marriage bed but in all the areas of our relationship. Show us how to love one another in such a way that neither of us will be tempted by the enemy. Let us honor You and strengthen our marriage through our physical relationship with one another. Amen.

## RECOMMENDED RESOURCES

*He's Just Not Up for It Anymore* by Bob Berkowitz and Susan Yager-Berkowitz

*How We Love* by Milan and Kay Yerkovich

*Intimacy Ignited: Conversations Couple to Couple* by Joseph and Linda Dillow; Peter and Lorraine Pintus

*Intimate Issues: 21 Questions Women Ask About Sex* by Linda Dillow and Lorraine Pintus

*Love and Respect* by Dr. Emerson Eggerichs

*Passionate Marriage: Keeping Love and Intimacy Alive in Committed Relationships* by David Schnarch

*Sheet Music* by Dr. Kevin Lehman

*The Five Love Languages* by Gary Chapman

*The Sex-Starved Marriage* by Michele Weiner-Davis

*The Sex-Starved Wife* by Michele Weiner-Davis

# Chapter 10

# I Struggle with Sexual Addiction

*A note to the reader:*
*This chapter addresses aspects of women's sexuality not normally discussed in a Christian context. You might find it unusual or even a little uncomfortable to see such topics addressed openly. Please know that I would not have included this chapter if I didn't see such a strong need for it. I encourage you to read on, finding support if you struggle in this area, compassion for others if you don't.*

It is so common for people to talk about men struggling with lust and sexual sin. When I was a child, I was exposed to pornography. Now, for as long as I can remember, I have struggled with sexual thoughts, sexual promiscuity, and even masturbation. It is so hard because women do not talk about this. It is a terrible feeling to think you are such a freak because you are a woman and struggle with this.

✦ ✦ ✦

Porn is not just "every man's battle." It's some women's
battle too. Hearing about sexual problems involving porn
as if it is just a male problem makes me feel like I'm a freak
of nature—a woman dealing with a man's problem. Shame
on top of shame.

Of all the subjects we're covering in this book, I have to say that
the least talked-about in Christian literature is this one: wom-
en's struggles with pornography, masturbation, and lust. Programs
such as Every Man's Battle workshops have addressed men's issues
with porn and blasted the lid off *that* secret—but nobody is talking
about it when it comes to women.

Make no mistake: our warped culture has ensured that women,
like men, are struggling with sexual issues. Remember the Secrets
Blog I told you about? In terms of sheer numbers, women reporting
addiction to pornography and/or masturbation represented the *second highest* number of responses. These were about equally divided
between married and unmarried women.

Phew! That's a lot to process.

My heart goes out to all the women who have been suffering alone
in their guilt and confusion. In this chapter, I hope to offer you some
reassurance that you are not a freak (as so many women who wrote
me referred to themselves) and that you are loved unconditionally by
God even in the face of this battle.

---

## Unlocking the Secret

Among the women who wrote me about this subject, I noticed several clear similarities:

- Tremendous guilt and shame for the behavior, along with
  the inability to stop it.

♦ Profound frustration that they've never seen it addressed in a Christian context except in relation to men.

♦ Exposure to pornography as a child, and/or remembering innocently masturbating as a child (and continuing through the adult years).

♦ Viewing porn on the Internet.

♦ Confusion over whether self-pleasuring is a sin.

♦ Deep fear of anyone finding out. More than any other secret, the women said things like, "This is the first time I've ever shared this with anyone."

♦ Extreme language when referring to themselves—for example, as a freak.

Because sexual addiction is such a deep, dark secret, we have no way of knowing exactly how many Christian women are dealing with it—and we probably never will. One estimate puts it at 3 percent of all adult women (compared to 8 percent of adult men), which would be about eight million women.[1] I think it's fair to say that whatever the number, it's likely increasing as we speak. Internet pornography is just as available to women as it is to men; primetime television programs are moving closer and closer to soft-core porn; secular romance novels are highly erotic as well. Never has sex been so out in the open, luring us in and twisting our minds. And the sexual behavior that takes place in response to this culture—usually while alone—tends to bring an avalanche of shame on those who become trapped.

## KEEPING THE SECRET

Unlike some of the other secrets we're discussing in this book, there is no mystery about why this one is kept in the dark.

> Women have problems with pornography too. Sometimes I wonder if I am the only one.

✦ ✦ ✦

> I wish I heard more about women with sexual addictions
> such as masturbation and porn and how to deal with them.
> Most of what I see is only from a male perspective.

To look at the available resources, you'd think this was only a problem for men and teenage boys. Consequently, women have never had any safe forum in which to discuss it. They've never been able to air out these thoughts, feelings, and experiences; they've never been able to get another's perspective on it. They've never even been able to objectively examine this experience and try to understand it. Consequently, it makes sense that they feel trapped and unable to change their situation.

Further compounding the secretive nature of these sexual issues is the fact that many Christians believe masturbation is a heinous sin, far greater than any other sin they may be committing (such as coveting or pride).

> I'm a Christian and have been for all my life. Somehow I
> know *this one act* breaks the Father's heart!

The guilt we experience when we believe we are regularly and repeatedly "breaking God's heart" is enormous. No wonder this came up as so many women's most pressing secret.

## THINK ABOUT IT

We were all created by God to be sensual beings. Our bodies experience pleasurable physical sensations; a caress on the cheek, a vigorous back rub, or a foot massage can produce wonderful feelings. At some point in our lives, usually in early childhood, we discover that our bodies can produce even more intense feelings—really good ones. Our sexuality awakens, and though we have no words for it and no context to understand it, we realize that we can touch ourselves in certain ways that produce pleasure. Developmentally, this is a normal period of discovery wherein children become aware of the sensations of their bodies.

The Bible tells us our bodies, our inmost beings, were created by God. We were knit together in our mothers' wombs. We can praise the Creator because we are fearfully and wonderfully made (Ps. 139:13–14). All aspects of our bodies, minds, and hearts are known by Him, and He intended us to know ourselves—to live in and feel our bodies.

Learning about these sensations isn't a bad thing; it's a normal part of learning how our bodies work. Adults in our lives are usually quick to put limits on any self-pleasuring behaviors. Families with healthy attitudes about sex put boundaries on the behavior and begin to talk honestly (and age-appropriately) with the children about their bodies. Some parents, however, actively discourage touching the "private parts" or even scold the children, beginning right away to instill guilt and shame about our natural, God-given sexuality.

This early experimentation with our bodies, along with appropriate teaching, helps us develop healthy sexual boundaries and behaviors as we mature into adults. Unfortunately, far too many children have their healthy development interrupted by exposure to our culture's warped sexual attitudes. Either they come across pornography, which leads them to masturbation and obsession with sex; or an adult in their lives crosses sexual/body boundaries, interfering with development of healthy sexual attitudes. Some people may not even remember any specific incident but may have been exposed to a highly sexualized environment or a hidden but highly charged undercurrent of sexuality in the family. Today, kids can watch regular television any time of day and receive far more sexual images than is appropriate for them. So it's not surprising that as adults, many find themselves dealing with inappropriate lust, pornography viewing, and self-pleasuring. What started out as a healthy progression was corrupted.

In the past, almost all sexual addiction problems were related to some kind of abuse or corruption as a child. However, that's no longer true. The Internet has changed everything. People with no previous risk factors, people who would even be considered highly unlikely to ever be tempted by such things, are now falling victim to the Internet pornography trap. And the most *unlikely* people, of course, are women.

If you're struggling with this issue, I want you to realize that it isn't happening because you are bad or because you're not a good Christian. It's most likely because somewhere along the way—whether in childhood or more recently—your normal, healthy sexual development was distorted by our sexually depraved culture. Then you made a series of unhealthy and, yes, sinful choices that eventually became an addiction. Please realize you are not alone in this, and there is help.

Our sexuality is God-given and a precious gift, albeit one we're told (in the Bible) is to be used under certain circumstances. Sexual feelings themselves are not wrong; they're a sign that our bodies are working and that we're alive. Instead of shaming ourselves, we can thank God for this aliveness in us. However, it's when we act on them in ungodly ways that we get into trouble.

Dr. Daniel Amen, in his book *Sex on the Brain*, talked about the differences between men's and women's brains. Because of these differences beginning at conception (too numerous to mention here), it sets us up to approach our struggles, even the same struggles, from different angles. Stereotypes come out of these gender-specific behaviors. We approach our desires differently. In general, we women are less impulsive—but we think along more emotional lines, are more sensitive to social cues and taboos, and can multitask while overthinking and overtalking everything. Men are more singular in their focus and in need of greater stimulation. Hence the stereotype for men regarding sex—sex is both stimulating and allows them to focus on one thing.[2]

These differences and the related male/female hormones affect how our sexuality is inwardly motivated and outwardly handled.

People with sexual addiction of both sexes, however, have similarities in decreased activity in the part of the brain that affects judgment and need for increased stimulation. All this to say, women and men are not hardwired exactly the same. We women have more layers to our sexual and emotional lives that make the problem less simplistic or obvious. But women struggle with longings in their sexual and emotional lives, and our culture is contributing to a rise in sexual addictions in women.

When women look at pornographic images, their bodies respond with arousal (just as men's bodies do). From a purely physical stand-point, that's an expected and natural response. It's usually a pleasurable experience (despite any guilt or shame), and psychologically, we're wired to want to repeat pleasurable experiences. The addiction factor of pornography and self-stimulation arises from this perfectly natural desire to repeat pleasant sensations. Some researchers have suggested that there is a biological component related to the sexual release obtained from masturbation. People become addicted to the brain's neurochemical response, much the same way one becomes addicted to the brain's response to mood-altering drugs. This is one of the reasons this problem is difficult (if not impossible) to solve on your own. Most Christian therapists view sexual addiction as *both* a sinful choice and a biological disease.[3]

## Spiritual Secrets

The Bible teaches that sexual relations are appropriate within mar-riage, not appropriate outside of it. However, some people take that to mean that since we're good Christians, we shouldn't ever have any sexual feelings outside of marriage. Of course, this is unrealistic, since we wouldn't be human if we didn't.

Sex outside of marriage is wrong. But sexuality is not wrong.

It's an important distinction. Within this framework, we can begin to explore the fine line between simply experiencing our sexual selves and behaving inappropriately.

From a Christian perspective, not all situations involving masturbation are the same. It is important to note that nowhere does
Scripture say that masturbation is a sin. In fact the word *masturbation* is not mentioned in the Bible. You may be a single woman
dealing with normal sexual feelings and have no marriage relationship in which to satisfy those desires. You might explore your feelings
and sensations through self-stimulation, seeking to know yourself
better. This is different than if you're a married woman using self-
stimulation either instead of or in addition to relations with your
husband. It's also different than if you are compulsively doing this,
or if you're using any kind of pornography to satisfy yourself.

An important distinction is what's going on in your mind, about
which the Bible does have something to say. We are told to keep our
minds pure and free from lust (Prov. 15:26; Phil. 4:8). Are you engaging in erotic fantasy? Are you stimulating your lustful feelings through
pornographic imagery? Or are you simply relieving your physical
need without fantasy or images?

There are varying viewpoints on this, but I'm going to go out
on a limb and say that the first thing you need to do is identify if
your personal situation is indeed sinful, and what makes it so. Lust
and use of pornography are clearly sins; any kind of sexual activity
done compulsively (i.e., with the inability to stop or control yourself) is a sin.

However, occasionally masturbation can be viewed as a wisdom
issue between you and God—that is, something the individual can
pray about while studying biblical truth and seeking God's will. The
Bible clearly says lust is a sin. Using pornographic images and/or
engaging in erotic fantasy is lust, so those activities are sinful. But
perhaps a single woman with a high sex drive needs to express her
sexuality instead of repress it. (Repression prior to marriage can lead
to serious sexual hang-ups once you get married.) It's possible she
might be able to express her sexuality by exploring her body while
thanking God for her health, her vitality, and her pleasurable sensations (as opposed to fantasizing or viewing porn).

If you are a single woman with a powerful sex drive, you may be tempted to get into illicit sexual relationships simply for a release. Perhaps with the right frame of mind, self-stimulation might be an answer for you to help avoid that. But only if you completely give it over to God, ask Him if it's the right thing for you, and keep your mind free of lust. The key is where you let your mind go.

Many theologians and pastors would disagree with me on this; and I want to make it clear that there are few situations that actually fit the "non-sinful" scenario I've described. However, if you are a single woman, not using erotic imagery, and not compulsive about it, then you probably don't have a true sexual addiction, so some of the information in this chapter might not apply to you. *Please pray about this*, and proceed carefully. If you cannot continue your behavior without guilt, then use the recommendations in this chapter to stop the behavior and move toward healing.

If you are married, there are strong biblical and psychological reasons to avoid solo sexual activity and, instead, deal with those feelings in the context of your marital relationship. As we discussed in the previous chapter, the physical aspect of marriage is a fundamental way that husbands and wives stay connected, express their love, and tell each other, "You are the only one for me." If you are taking care of your own sexual needs without involving your husband, you are depriving your marriage of opportunities for increased closeness and intimacy. You might feel you have great reasons for doing so—your husband's lack of interest, or he doesn't know how to satisfy you, or you're simply not attracted to him. But taking care of it yourself is a way of avoiding or denying those problems; it does nothing to solve them. I encourage you to get real about what's going on, stop rationalizing the behavior, and begin looking at ways to actually improve your situation rather than continue to avoid it.

Let's take into account the whole realm of healthy sexuality and remember that sex is just one aspect of it. This is especially good news for singles. Healthy sexuality is also about feeling connected to our bodies and enjoying our bodies in a variety of ways. Enjoying the movement of our bodies through dance or athletics, exercising our bodies and allowing the circulation to enliven us, being in touch with our femininity, dressing for an occasion, feeling pretty and confident in who God made us to be—all are part of our sexual being.

What if your secret struggle is same-sex attraction? You are a Christian, and you refuse to abandon your faith to embrace a lesbian lifestyle. You may not even consider yourself gay. You may have never had a physical encounter with another woman but can't stop fantasizing about the idea of it. Or there is a same-sex fling in your past that haunts you. You could be married or single and still struggle with these thoughts. Telling someone is the last thing you could imagine yourself doing, especially girlfriends who might start treating you differently or feel uncomfortable in your presence. Yet you find yourself lingering over Victoria's Secret catalogs. You may find women more emotionally compatible and have difficulty relating to men, or you have been hurt by men and distrust them. You may have had a woman subtly sexualize your friendship and find yourself aroused by this forbidden attention. Whatever your situation, these feelings can be real and problematic for you.

Through the years I have seen women in my clinical practice struggle painfully with all of these issues—everything from self-stimulation to Internet porn to lesbian fantasies.

> I have struggled with sexual addiction, masturbation, and being attracted to women. I felt so much shame about myself and as a Christian woman and preacher's kid, this was beyond embarrassing. It has been a long road with many obstacles and hurts to work through. Freedom for me has come through working and sharing with my therapist and a few close friends to get to a place of acceptance of my problem. But it is an ongoing process that I must always keep in check. With support I can now go to the beach and see children playing instead of women's breasts. Knowing what my weakness is and accepting its limita-

tions has helped me come out of my shame and is the very
thing God has used to make me stronger.

I am covering a wide range of sexual behaviors here. You need to be
honest with yourself and determine where you are on this spectrum.
Ask yourself, Under what circumstances do I turn to self-pleasuring
or sexual-related behaviors or attractions? Are there similar themes,
feelings, or patterns when these desires arise? It can be difficult to
know whether you're simply guilty of occasional lust or you have a
full-blown addiction. If you have suffered guilt and shame over your
behavior and have tried to stop the behavior but haven't been able to,
you may be addicted. Or, for example, if you are using self-pleasuring
to the point of hurting your body physically but still can't stop, addiction is almost certain.

It's important to acknowledge this addiction because it gives you
the power to begin approaching it successfully. Please be clear about
one thing: most people have *no success* trying to recover from addiction alone. Without confession, support, and accountability to
another person, there's not much chance of healing.

What if you clearly know that your sexual addiction is sinful and
harmful, and yet you can't seem to stop? I recommend you start with
the following steps:

+ Pray and *thank God* for your healthy body. Praise Him for
  the glorious way He has designed you and the wonderful
  feelings your body is capable of having.

+ Repent of your behavior. Take complete responsibility for
  giving in to temptation without blaming anyone else
  (including the Internet). Acknowledge that you have used
  God's gift wrongly, and make a clear decision that you no
  longer want to do this.

+ Confess your sin, and ask God's forgiveness. Then *accept*
  that you are forgiven . . . no exceptions.

- Ask for God's wisdom and guidance to break free from this bondage. Ask Him to reveal to you any falsehoods in your thinking. Commit to Him that you will follow where He leads.

- Reflect on the times and situations in which you are drawn into your sexual behavior. Be aware of the feelings that are present right before the sexual feelings ignite. This will give you a clue as to what your true longings are underneath your sexual desire. It may take a bit of effort to become aware and pinpoint those feelings, since sexual desire can override the underlying feelings.

- Ask yourself if this is the best way to deal with your emotional longings. Then seek appropriate options to address your true need(s).

- Whenever you feel tempted, or if you succumb, verbally rebuke the enemy. Tell him he might win a skirmish, but he'll never win the war because God has already won. Ban the enemy from your life.

- Begin to consider ways you can change your environment or your schedule that will lead to fewer opportunities for temptation. There may be places you have to avoid.

- Monitor your media consumption, and be ruthless about eliminating anything that stimulates your sexual feelings. This can include television programs, magazines, books, movies, and even music.

- Look at some of the resources (listed at the end of this chapter) that give detailed explanations, from varying viewpoints, about how to break free of lust issues.

As with all addictions, there will be no movement toward healing without first taking complete responsibility and truly repenting.

The most important thing I can tell you is that this sin is not higher up on the sin hierarchy than others. It's *not* unforgivable—so repent, ask forgiveness, and accept that you will be forgiven. Even if you're still yielding to sexual temptation, it's crucial you ask forgiveness every time, and understand that God does not love you any less. Romans 8:1 says, "Therefore, there is now no condemnation for those who are in Christ Jesus." You do not have to live in your shame. As you are looking for ways to change your life and be freed from this bondage, remember that you are already free in Christ. You are forgiven. You are not alone.

## From Secrets to Solutions

One of the letters written in to the Secrets Blog contained some valuable insights:

> I have only shared my secret with one other person, my sister. I had to tell someone because I knew it would take the power out of what I was doing if someone else knew. My secret is I was addicted to viewing and thinking about pornography. I felt so ashamed for doing this behind my husband's back, but I could not stop. I don't understand what was going on with me. Once I shared this embarrassing act with my sister, I have not done it since. With daily prayer it has been two months that I have not had a desire to look at any porn. Do other women struggle with this?

I am so glad this woman wrote me because she has realized two significant things: (1) that sharing our secret with someone else can loosen its hold over us, and (2) that daily prayer—sharing the secret with God—can be a key to changing everything.

*Be honest with yourself.* You may be in the habit of trying not to think about this dark side of your life. But I want you to think about it. Ask yourself, When did this start? Was there a precipitating circumstance? What are the triggers that usually start this behavior? Is there anything about my habits or environment that I can immediately change to lessen the temptation? It's time to stop avoiding it and start looking directly at this behavior.

*Be honest with God.* Confess everything to God. Lay it out for Him as you understand it, and ask Him to show you the things that you can't see. Tell Him you want to be rid of this secret. As I said in the previous section, you can pray for forgiveness, thank God for your body, and ask Him to protect you from the enemy. Sometimes we are not ready to give up a secret problem, and we avoid talking to God because we are afraid He will actually hear our prayer and take the problem from us. We can become fearful and conflicted, opting for the immediate gratification of something known rather than allowing Him to meet us where we are in our pain. Tell Him about your shame, describe to Him any anger, and tell Him if you know you *should* stop this behavior but you don't really *want* to. You've got to start by being totally straightforward about where you are. Begin a dialogue with God, and let it continue—several times a day if possible—as long as you still struggle.

*Be honest with a trusted person—friend, family member, or therapist.* This may be the most difficult part, but it is absolutely crucial. One of the ways you can demonstrate your sincere repentance is by confessing aloud to another person. Start by praying, asking God who you should talk to about this problem. Be sure to choose someone who will love and accept you rather than judge your behavior. When you find the person, share in the way that feels most comfortable to you, asking for prayer support. Your goal is, as the letter writer said, to "take the power out" of your secret.

*Seek out a support group.* Because of the nature of sexual addiction and how easy it is to slide back into it (because the enemy is so strong in this area), I highly recommend you find a sexual addiction recovery group. Continual accountability is essential! I've listed some resources at the end of this chapter, both Christian and secular. You might be surprised at how many groups exist.

This whole book is about bringing our secrets out of the dark, removing their destructive power in our lives. This secret may be the *most* difficult to share, and yet ironically, it is the one that *most requires* you to share it in order to defeat it. I encourage you to explore all the resources listed at the end of this chapter—books, Web sites, and programs—and find a safe place to begin dealing honestly with this secret.

## Praying Scripture for Your Secret

Pray Psalm 18:16–17, 19.

Heavenly Father, the Psalmist wrote, "[The Lord] reached down from on high and took hold of me; he drew me out of deep waters. He rescued me from my powerful enemy, from my foes, who were too strong for me. He brought me out into a spacious place; he rescued me because he delighted in me." Father, I ask that You would rescue me in the same way, that You would draw me from these waters that threaten to drown me. Save me from my enemies, Lord. They are too strong for me, but not for You. I know You delight in me, and I thank You for Your awesome love and protection. Amen.

## Recommended Resources

There aren't many books that address the issues of lust, pornography, and masturbation for adult women. However, there are quite a few Christian books that have some perspective on these issues (even though often aimed at men or teens) that will help you to understand them more deeply and, more importantly, give you the tools to break free.

### Books
*Desires in Conflict: Answering the Struggle for Sexual Identity* by Joe Dallas
*Every Woman's Battle* by Shannon Ethridge
*Healing the Wounds of Sexual Addiction* by Mark R. Laaser
*I Surrender All* by Clay and Renee Cross

*In the Shadows of the Net: Breaking Free from Compulsive Online
    Sexual Behavior* by Patrick Carnes, David L. Delmonico,
    Elizabeth Griffin, Joseph M. Moriarity
*Life's Healing Choices* by John Baker
*Masturbation: What You Should Know to Know How to Help* by
    Richard Thomas
*Sex and the Supremacy of Christ* by John Piper
*Sex Is Not the Problem (Lust Is)* by Joshua Harris
*Sexual Happiness in Marriage* by Herbert J. Miles
*Tangled in the Web: Understanding Cybersex from Fantasy to
    Addiction* by Kimberly S. Young
*The Final Freedom: Pioneering Sexual Addiction Recovery* by Douglas
    Weiss
*The Struggle* by Steve Gerali

## ARTICLES

"Help for the Sexually Desperate," *Christianity Today* 52, no. 3
    (March 2008): 28; available at www.christianitytoday.com/
    ct/2008/march/18.28.html

## ORGANIZATIONS

Celebrate Recovery—www.celebraterecovery.com
    A Christian organization with conferences, local groups, books,
    and other resources
Sex and Love Addicts Anonymous—www.slaafws.org
    A traditional, secular twelve-step program with local chapters
    in hundreds of cities
Heart to Heart Counseling Center—www.sexaddict.com
    719-278-3708
Pure Desire Ministry International—www.puredesire.org

*Part Four*

# SECRETS ABOUT OUR INNER LIVES

# Chapter 11

# I'm Discontented with Life

I secretly hate my life. I love my kids, but I REALLY HATE MY LIFE.

+ + +

At middle age, I feel like I haven't reached some of my "ideals" in the way I imagined. Life just seems pretty pointless.

+ + +

I secretly wish I could go back to my senior year of high school and live my life all over again.

+ + +

I continually daydream of a better life. One with more

money, where I am able to do anything I want. I have even been daydreaming about having another husband who treats me better. I know this isn't what God wants, but it is truly hard not to do it.

Back when I was in high school, the yearbook had a section in which all the seniors listed their goals for the future. Some of them said they wanted to attend a certain university or have a particular career. Others were more specific and said they "wanted to marry Jason and have three children," or maybe they wanted to "travel the world." But the one thing I remember as being the most universal statement from the graduating seniors was "I want to be happy."

Of course, there's nothing wrong with being happy; it definitely beats the alternative! But even back then, I wondered if *happiness* really counted as a legitimate goal in life. How do people strive to be happy, and how do they know when they've succeeded? Today I see the results of our generation's single-minded pursuit of happiness, and the sad truth is that most people find it agonizingly elusive.

---

## Unlocking the Secret

Meredith is in her forties, has been married more than twenty years, and has two children in high school. She feels her life is meaningless. "It's crazy, but I fear that *this is all there is.* If I could just escape the marriage and kids, I would have no responsibilities and be free and happy. I know it's not realistic. Sometimes I can't stand to live with them—and then again, I can't make it without them."

Our Secrets Blog revealed numerous stories like Meredith's, along with other kinds of discontent. Many reported a vague feeling of "Is this all there is?" like Meredith. Others wrote that they fantasize about a different life—usually with a better husband, more money, or a life without kids and responsibility. A few wrote simply, "I am unhappy."

Beyond the women who wrote specifically about their discontent or disillusionment were the many other secrets that convey, by their very existence, a degree of unhappiness. Having a secret implies something negative, shameful, or embarrassing is plaguing us—decreasing our sense of contentment or joy in life.

So how is it that so many of us carry around so much dissatisfaction? The fact that we live in the wealthiest and most privileged society in the history of the world yet experience epidemic levels of discontent is mind-boggling! So much so that the topic of happiness has been studied intensely over the last few decades by psychologists, social scientists, philosophers, and even theologians. Everyone is asking the same question: Why is there so much *unhappiness* in the midst of so much plenty? Scholars from each of these disciplines have uncovered astonishingly similar answers, which I will try to summarize in the rest of this chapter and help you apply their discoveries to finding healing in your own life. To put it simply, our level of unhappiness has to do with (1) our expectations about how life is supposed to be, (2) our acceptance of reality or lack thereof, and (3) where we choose to focus—inwardly on self, or outwardly on God and others.

In some ways, our levels of discontent are specifically related to our current culture, with its emphasis on consumerism and technology and our expectation of wealth. But the idea of discontent is also timeless and has been a problem for people throughout the ages. Matthew Henry, an eighteenth-century clergyman famous for his verse-by-verse commentary on the Bible, said this:

> Discontent is a sin that is its own punishment and makes men torment themselves; it makes the spirit sad, the body sick, and all the enjoyments sour; it is the heaviness of the heart and the rottenness of the bones. It is a sin that is its own parent. It arises not from the condition, but from the mind. As we find Paul contented in a prison, so Ahab was discontented in a palace.[1]

Henry pointed out what psychologists see in their offices every day—that discontent, once it takes hold, invades your entire being and robs you of the ability to enjoy life or see the good in anything. He also noted that discontent arises "not from the condition, but from the mind." And today's researchers, for all their expertise, haven't been able to improve upon that assessment.

## KEEPING THE SECRET

If so many of us are unhappy, why is it such a big secret?

Tanya is a gorgeous woman with a successful career, a beautiful home, and three well-adjusted children. She is known and respected throughout her industry and is well acquainted with designer clothes and accessories. But when she's alone in her kitchen with the granite countertops and professional ovens, she looks around and wonders, *Why am I not happy?* She finds herself daydreaming about escaping this life—just picking up and running away like a rebellious teenager. At the same time, she doesn't understand this desperate desire. Shouldn't she be satisfied? She's done everything a woman can do to achieve success—and she's done it all while being devoted to God. She prays regularly, attends church, and even leads a Bible study. But it still seems as though something's missing, and she doesn't know what it is. What she *does* know is that she can't share these thoughts with anyone. They'd think she was crazy! She has it all—she has no right to want more.

We keep secrets because we're ashamed, or we think something about us is *not okay*. In our culture, it's definitely not okay to be unhappy, especially if externally your life appears blessed. Happiness has been shown time and time again to be the number one goal of most Americans, and it's also the most important goal parents have for their children. Often I hear people discussing their children's futures, and they'll say, "It doesn't matter to me what kind of career they have—I just want them to be happy." Does that sound familiar? I admit I've even had these thoughts myself.

Our country was founded on a conviction that each one of us has a God-given *right* to life, liberty, and the pursuit of happiness. Never mind the fact that the Founding Fathers' definition of *happiness* was something completely different from how we define it today (I'll get to that in a bit), we Americans were raised with a hefty sense of entitlement. It's the American dream. We all *deserve* to be happy, and if we're not, there must be something wrong with us.

You look around and know that you're blessed if you have a roof over your head and food on the table, yet you also know you're not satisfied, and you're ashamed of yourself. You hear your parents' voices in your head reminding you how grateful you should be and how lucky you are. You don't understand why you can't be happy with what you have. The shame leads you to keep it a secret. *What would others think if they knew how miserable I am?*

Perhaps the worst part of this embarrassment is that, like Tanya, you don't know *why* you're unhappy, and you have no clue how to change it. It's extremely frustrating. You might be able to identify some things in your life that could be improved, but they don't seem like enough to warrant this pervasive sense of restlessness, of wishing you were someone else or somewhere else. You keep it a secret because you try not to think about it; if you did, you wouldn't be able to adequately name it or explain it. The dissatisfaction has crept up on you—you have no idea when it even started. But now it's like a low-grade fever, making you feel rotten all the time. You don't know why you have it, and you certainly have no idea how to get rid of it. Under these circumstances, it's no wonder you carry your discontent around as a secret.

## THINK ABOUT IT

In Abraham Maslow's Hierarchy of Needs theory, he talks about our most basic needs—food, shelter, clothing—as being our first level of concern. As each level of need is met, we move up the pyramid from basic to more esoteric and existential needs, such as art, culture, meaning, and value. It's a given that if your stomach is grumbling, you probably don't care to spend your time at the latest art exhibit. The irony of this life is that the more we have at our fingertips to satisfy us, the less satisfied we are. As Solomon said in the book of Ecclesiastes, "Everything is meaningless" (1:2).

In the early 1990s, I had the wonderful privilege of visiting the former Soviet Union soon before and right after the fall of communism. I was amazed at how litter-less Russia was, for without capitalism there were no ad campaigns or direct-mail marketing brochures lining the streets. No wonder they were hungry for Bible handouts—there was not much in print at all. We were so excited to bring back with us two young teenage Christian girls, who had served as our translators, and show them the wonders of the U.S. and the freedom of perhaps studying at a Christian university. I'll never forget taking them to the grocery store for the first time to get food that they might like, asking them to pick out a box of cereal and watching their look of utter shock. I thought I was going to lose them right there in the cereal aisle! Instead of being a treat, it overwhelmed them to the point of feeling paralyzed. Their response was not joy. Distraught, they said, "You have too many choices; it makes our head dizzy, and we don't know what to do." As you can imagine, they taught me as much if not more than I taught them. More is not always better; it's just more.

During times of war (World War II, Desert Storm) or times of disaster (9/11) or universal hardship (the Great Depression), people band together more, feel more benevolent, rally behind the cause, or have a greater sense of purpose even though life may be more difficult. Misery really does love company. We long for better times and an easier life, but it seems that the hope—not the actual getting there—is what is most meaningful. When we are most comfortable, we can fall into being less real, less in touch with what's important, and less connected to others. We hide behind what were supposed to be our dreams come true. How can we tell others they are not?

My secret is that sometimes I think about what it would be like to chuck it all and not have to worry about anyone but myself.

＋ ＋ ＋

I love my husband and children, but I sometimes secretly think it would be so simple to make my own decisions and not be tied down.

It's no secret that we live in a *me*-obsessed culture. The fact that we're in a consumer-based society, bombarded by advertising messages 24/7, has created an environment in which we are encouraged—no, *expected*—to think about our own personal gratification constantly. *Do I need a new car? Maybe I should take a vacation to the Caribbean. Will my clothes survive the fashion police?* Or, like many of the women I heard from, *Would I be happier in a different life?*

This focus on *me* is the key to understanding how our culture defines *happiness* today. We think of happiness as a pleasurable feeling, a state of well-being that is completely self-contained. Our happiness comes and goes as events and circumstances shape each day. If we *feel* happy for most of each day, we think we are living the good life. Happiness is all about *how I feel*.

But this type of happiness—the good feelings that are determined by our circumstances—doesn't last. Let's say you decide to spend a day at the mall with your girlfriends, and you find some amazing designer clothes in just your size with huge markdowns. You go crazy! When all is said and done, you've spent two hundred dollars but ended up with two thousand dollars' worth of gorgeous tops, pants, and jackets. You are ecstatic. Once home, you try on all your clothes again, admire them in the mirror, and bask in the happy feelings of your good fortune. Soon it's time to pick up the kids from school, and of course they are squabbling in the car, taking the edge off that blissful glow you had going. Then you find out your fourth-grader has a giant project due tomorrow that he hasn't even started, and you're going to be up half the night. Soon it's time for dinner, and you realize that in the excitement of the mall-crawl, you neglected to pick up anything from the grocery store. It's barely a few hours after the victorious shopping excursion had you on cloud nine, and now you're completely down in the dumps. Once again, you can't believe this is your life. Where did your happiness go?

Doesn't it seem as though this kind of fleeting happiness is not really worth much? Sure, it's fun, and it definitely has its place. But how do we find a deeper sense of contentment—*joy,* if you will—that stays with us through the ups and downs of life?

Throughout recorded history up until the current baby boom generation, people had a definition of *happiness* or *contentment* that looked very different from ours. Rather than being a pleasurable feeling or a fleeting glimpse of satisfaction, the ancients viewed happiness as "a life well lived, a life of virtue and character, a life that manifests wisdom, kindness and goodness."[2] It was expected that this type of life naturally brought with it a deep sense of well-being.

Take a moment to consider this definition. Maybe you're unclear on what it really means. We certainly don't talk that way these days. (When was the last time you heard a commercial promoting kindness and goodness?) The ideas of virtue and character barely enter into our thinking—all the other details of life are just too time-consuming, aren't they? People who came before us had much different lives, far less luxury, and far more hard work, so they learned to cultivate a kind of joy that persists even through hardship.

Now we live in an era in which the focus is on doing as little work as possible, making as much money as possible, having the nicest things, the best vacations, and being the most attractive person in the room. If we meet all those criteria, then by our society's standards, we should be happy.

Jennifer Hecht's book, *The Happiness Myth,* is a fascinating historical and sociological analysis of happiness throughout the ages. It describes how each culture and era sets the expectations for what *should* produce happiness, and these expectations may or may not bear any resemblance to reality. That is, what the culture *expects* will produce happiness may in fact produce something totally different. Hecht wrote, "Our era believes that happiness requires a particular relationship to physical exercise, legal and illegal drugs, food, public decorum, sexual normality, and material and media culture. It [our era] has no more claim to truth on these matters than any other . . . The basic modern assumptions about how to be happy are nonsense."[3]

It might be hard to admit, but if we look at ourselves and look at those around us, we can't help but know this is true.

Our culture has produced huge expectations in us—assumptions that we *should* be able to accomplish certain society-defined goals, and that these accomplishments will make us happy. There are two big problems here: (1) we may not reach those goals set by our culture, and (2) even if we do, they won't make us happy.

## Meeting Expectations

Part of our maturing process as adults and as Christians is learning to take a look at the expectations we've developed and assess how realistic they are. One of the first things you can do if you're trying to understand your discontent is to ask yourself, What was I expecting?

Most of us expected some sort of "happily ever after" once we married our Prince Charming. We were never adequately prepared for the challenges of marriage. This, I think, is one of the biggest culprits in our marriage-related unhappiness. The difference between our dream and our reality is maddening. If our expectations had been vastly different—if they had included knowledge of how very difficult it can be to live for a lifetime with another person, and if they had prepared us to see the purpose of marriage differently—then we would respond to the realities of marriage very differently. As it is, we look at marriage from a me-centered position just as our culture tells us. We go into it feeling "in love" and having visions of our personal happiness with this man. Rarely do larger issues enter our consciousness: marriage as a spiritual discipline, for example, or marriage as our responsibility to the larger society.

## Accepting Reality

Marriage is just one example, but the concept applies to all the areas of our lives. Thus one of our tasks as we mature through adulthood is to begin to look at the difference between our expectations and reality, and then to begin cultivating a healthy acceptance of reality.

"Life is difficult," wrote M. Scott Peck as the first line to his famous book, *The Road Less Traveled*. His point was that until we accept the truth of that statement, we will never find a sense of peace or contentment in this life.[4] As long as our *expectation* is that life should be easy and fun all the time, then the discrepancy between our expectation and the harshness of this difficult life will cause us ongoing discontent and a pervasive lack of joy.

Many of us have a wake-up call around our forties when we suddenly realize *this is it. This is my life.* The thought that comes after that is often, *Is this all there is?* If you're having those thoughts, it's probably because your expectations didn't accurately portray what reality was going to be like. You have a choice when you reach this crossroad. You can go into despair or spin out of control—create for yourself a classic midlife crisis. Or you can begin to look at the pieces of your life and discover how your faulty expectations set you up for this rude awakening.

As adults, we often forget that we are still "growing up." When discontent sets in, it's a sign that there is more maturing to do, more acceptance of reality, more growth.

## Spiritual Secrets

Generations who came before us seemed to instinctually understand that the key to contentment was not in daily fun or good feelings but in living life for something larger and more important than the self—usually God, family, and country. They understood that you can *pursue* being a good person—someone with character and integrity, someone who is caring and compassionate—but you can't really pursue happiness because it's so fleeting. The satisfaction that comes from living life *well* is a deep-seated kind of contentment that doesn't shift with the tides.

I think most of us know this somewhere, deep in our souls, whether or not we ever pay attention to it. There is an unconscious knowledge that the things we pursue, such as fun and fashion and a successful career, are not producing in us the satisfaction we crave. I think that's why the book *The Purpose Driven Life* by Rick Warren became such a huge bestseller—deep down, we know we need to find some kind of purpose to live for. We're afraid we're missing it, and we're right.

Strangely enough, even though we instinctively know we need to find a purpose for our lives, we fantasize about the opposite. We are so entrenched in the culture-defined view of happiness as a life of total leisure that many of us fantasize about "chucking it all," having no responsibilities and being able to completely control our destinies. We don't think about the fact that we're actually dreaming about a life with *nothing to live for*. If the fantasy came true, we wouldn't be any happier because what we truly need is the opposite—a life with something far more meaningful to live for than just *myself*. We need a purpose, something bigger than us.

That something is found in God and in the person of Jesus Christ. Jesus said, "Seek first [God's] kingdom and his righteousness, and all these things will be given to you as well" (Matt. 6:33). This is a simple statement of a complex truth: we cannot get the happiness we want by seeking it—but by seeking *God* and seeking to live a life of character and virtue as He would want.

I know women who are followers of Christ, yet they still feel they are missing out on the joy in life. Rob Bell wrote, "You can't be connected with God until you're at peace with who you are. If you're still upset that God gave you this body or this life or this family or these circumstances, you will never be able to connect with God in a healthy, thriving, sustainable sort of way. You'll be at odds with your maker."[5] Ask yourself, What am I unhappy about? Am I having trouble accepting my circumstances? You can begin to uncover the roots of your discontent. Then ask yourself, Do I truly believe God loves me and wants only the best for me? Often this is where we find we can only answer truthfully no, and we see where we need to begin our work. Identifying where your dissatisfaction begins can be a motivator to get up off the couch and start doing something about it.

## From Secrets to Solutions

Dealing with discontent is more than just a process of thinking things through and praying about it. It takes *action* to begin changing our orientation from a me focus to a God-and-others focus.

I'm hesitant to ask you to add one more thing to your to-do list because most women are stretched to the limit as it is. But I want to suggest that you at least spend some time honestly evaluating all the things you do in a day or a week. What is your motivation for what you do? Not what you tell yourself, but your *true motives* behind all the things you do. How much of your time do you spend checking things off a to-do list, not gaining any sense of satisfaction from them? Are you doing anything on a daily or weekly basis that is outward-focused—that is, serving someone besides you and your family?

You may be thinking, *I already live life for others—in fact, I have completely lost myself because I do everything for my family.* Some of you may have even crossed the line from your discontent into depression or despair because there is nothing of *you* left. In that case, the idea of outward focus may make you feel so completely misunderstood that you want to scream or give up entirely. Hold on—stay with me, and try not to lose heart. (We will get to depression in a following chapter, and, yes, there is hope.)

Many women get out of balance, not because they're focused exclusively on self but because they have an unhealthy focus on someone else as the primary motivator for their lives, usually their children and/or their husbands. Notice I said an *unhealthy* focus. This means you are living life *through* them, neglecting your responsibility to yourself, to God, and to the world at large. What we need to cultivate is a healthy level of focus on our own needs and spiritual growth, balanced with our responsibility to family and to the world.

If you're a mom, working your tail off morning until night with no energy left to think about the world, perhaps what might help is to reframe some of your duties and obligations. The time you spend raising your children, interacting with them, teaching them, and disciplining them is a ministry in the service of God *and* the world. Can you find more satisfaction in your daily life by recognizing Whom you are serving and the eternal value of what you're doing?

You may wonder why I keep talking about our responsibility to the *world*. It's because cultivating an outward focus, asking ourselves what we can do today to make the world a better place, is one of the most effective ways of getting out of the me trap and into a more healthy and contented frame of mind. Shifting our focus and perspective can make all the difference, whether our circumstances change or not. Internal shifts can cause profound change in our external outlook!

For a variety of excellent resources on discovering contentedness, see the list at the end of the chapter. Meanwhile, let's talk about getting rid of this secret.

*Be honest with yourself.* Take a few moments to identify your areas of discontent. What do you think is fueling it? Why do you keep this a secret? Now ask yourself what is the secret underneath the discontent—the one you are hiding from yourself? Is there something that pops into your consciousness every now and then but you always push it away? See if you can begin to understand your unhappiness a little better.

*Be honest with God.* Pray about your discontent, and ask God to begin revealing to you the possible reasons. If you are angry with life, tell Him. If you feel deeply disappointed, let Him know about it. Sometimes it helps to pray the Psalms—David was extremely good at expressing sorrow to God. He wasn't afraid to be honest about his feelings, his fears, his disappointments. The neat thing about David's lamenting psalms is that they almost always end with praise. David discovered a powerful truth: simply sharing our troubles candidly with God can lead us to a place of peace and acceptance, where we're able to praise God in the midst of whatever's going on.

*Be honest with someone else.* Depending on the depth of your unhappiness and whether it has progressed to actual depression, you may or may not need the help of a licensed, biblical counselor. But is there someone with whom you can share this secret? Talking with a trusted friend can help take the secrecy away and lift the burden. It can also show you that others feel much the same thing, and maybe you and your friend will be able to move forward together in searching for answers.

## PRAYING SCRIPTURE FOR YOUR SECRET

Pray Psalm 22:1–5.

> My God, my God, why have you forsaken me?
> Why are you so far from saving me,
> so far from the words of my groaning?
> O my God, I cry out by day, but you do not answer,
> by night, and am not silent.
> Yet you are enthroned as the Holy One;
> you are the praise of Israel.
> In you our fathers put their trust;
> they trusted and you delivered them.
> They cried to you and were saved;
> in you they trusted and were not disappointed.

Lord God, let me, like the Psalmist, put all my trust in You. Deliver me from this discontent. Show me the way, Lord. I am listening, and I will follow You. Amen.

## RECOMMENDED RESOURCES

*Holy Discontent: Fueling the Fire that Ignites Personal Vision* by Bill Hybels

*Reframe Your Life: Transforming Your Pain into Purpose* by Stephen Arterburn

*The Happiness Myth: Why What We Think Is Right Is Wrong* by Jennifer Hecht

*The Lost Virtue of Happiness* by J. P. Moreland and Klaus Issler

*The Myth of Happiness: Discovering a Joy You Never Thought Possible* by Rich Wagner

*The Secret to True Happiness: Enjoy Today, Embrace Tomorrow* by Joyce Meyer

# Chapter 12

# I Struggle with Spiritual Disconnect

I haven't read my Bible in quite some time, and I'm finding that I don't have a desire to do so. I just can't seem to
bring myself to pray or do anything. I want God to be
number one, but at the same time I don't want to do what
it takes to make Him number one . . . My motivation is
at an all-time low.

◆ ◆ ◆

I don't want to have to be the spiritual head of my house.
I want my husband to be! Why can't men realize they are
not doing their job? It puts a lot of pressure upon us. This
is not the way God designed it to be.

Jennifer became a Christian eight years ago, and she hit the
ground running. Her hunger for the Word was insatiable, and she

couldn't get enough of worship. Soon she was involved in several church ministries, going to a weekly Bible study, and listening to Christian music constantly on the radio. Meanwhile, her husband also became a Christian, and Jennifer was overjoyed. But soon she realized that her husband's idea of what it meant to be a Christian was vastly different from hers. While she looked at her conversion and baptism as a whole new start to life, he looked at it more like a one-time event. His perspective was, "I'm baptized. I'm saved. Done." He wasn't much interested in Bible study or anything else. As Jennifer began to learn more about the expectations her church had for Christian families, she became more and more disappointed. Her husband was not being "a good Christian," let alone aspiring to be the spiritual head of the household. Jennifer's excitement about her new spiritual life now had a downside—discord in her marriage.

---

## UNLOCKING THE SECRET

Numerous women wrote in to the Secrets Blog with spiritual issues, and they fell into three general categories: (1) problems with spiritual dryness or distance from God, (2) disappointment that their husbands don't aspire to be the spiritual leader in the family, and (3) spiritually unequal marriages in which the wife is a devoted follower of Christ, and the husband is either lukewarm or totally not interested. All of these represent some kind of disconnect in the faith journey, whether between self and God, or self and spouse.

When I talk with women about the issues involving their spiritual life, one thing I notice is that they tend to judge themselves, not on any sort of objective basis, but in comparison (we women are experts at comparison) to what they see around them. Actually, to what they *think* they see around them. If a woman is in the spiritual doldrums and can't get interested in prayer or worship, she looks around and sees other women who seem like Christian powerhouses. You know the ones—they are prayer warriors, and their passion for

Jesus shines brightly all the time. They *never* seem to falter in their faith.

If a woman is married and her husband isn't a biblical leader in the family or if he isn't even a believer, then all she can see are the "Christian couples" in church. She imagines each of those men as being a strong, caring, compassionate, godly husband, leading the family in daily prayer and weekly devotions. These women tend to idealize all the men they see in leadership roles, being especially vulnerable to having a crush on the pastor.

Assessing your own experience by what you see around you, however, doesn't give you an accurate picture, because the people around you are most likely not showing you all of themselves. Those prayer warrior ladies at church? You can bet they go through tough times with God. Those couples? Think about it for a second, and you'll realize that very few marriages are on the inside exactly as they appear on the outside. You have no idea how many of those men were dragged to church with a heavy silence in the car on the way.

So a big part of this secret is not only the spiritual disconnect you're experiencing but also the faulty messages you're receiving by looking around you and thinking everyone else has something you don't.

## KEEPING THE SECRET

Have you ever had the experience of sitting in Bible study or a small group of women, and everyone's talking about some biblical topic, and you become frustrated because it seems as if no one in the group is willing to take the gloves off and get *real*? It takes time and trust for a group to develop to the point where the members feel free to peel off the layers of their facades (which they usually don't even know they're wearing) and start admitting some of their not-so-Christian thoughts, feelings, and experiences. We are not willing to share our faults and foibles with just anyone.

This is the dynamic that keeps our spiritual issues a secret. We think everyone else is constantly experiencing a terrific relationship with God, and everyone else has a perfect Christian marriage, and we are the only ones who don't. We don't know what others are experiencing, and we assume we're the only ones who are somehow less spiritual. In that environment, of course we keep our spiritual secrets to ourselves!

When we are still growing into maturity as Christians, we have a hard time seeing the truth that all Christians have doubts, struggles, and sins and, more importantly, that those things don't negate our Christianity. We wrestle with a natural tendency to place everything in one camp: either good or bad. There are good Christians and bad Christians. We each want to be a good Christian, so we keep all the negatives a secret.

Do you remember the media circus that occurred when, ten years after her death, Mother Teresa's private writings became public? People were shocked that apparently Mother Teresa had experienced a deep darkness in her prayer life; for nearly fifty years she had continued to serve God and mankind and pray without ceasing even though it felt to her that God had stopped returning her calls. She wrestled with doubts and questions and pain as anyone would, but she kept serving, kept believing. This is incredibly difficult for many people to accept or understand. They want to believe that Mother Teresa was "all good," a true saint with no faults. A lack of spiritual understanding led many to believe that her doubts could not coexist with her faith—that, in fact, the darkness she experienced somehow canceled out the good she did by ministering to others in the service of Christ. Many people began to ask whether Mother Teresa was actually a hypocrite (someone who pretended to be something she was not). I don't know about you, but the idea of questioning the faith of Mother Teresa, of all people, seems unfathomable to me!

The point is that we keep our secrets because we ourselves aren't sure how to integrate our doubts, dryness, and failures into our picture of being a good Christian girl, and we know that others don't know how either. We're pretty sure others will begin to see us as bad people or bad Christians if we reveal ourselves. So we keep quiet.

## THINK ABOUT IT
### *If You Are in a Spiritual Desert*

Julie was a stay-at-home mom with a baby and a toddler. Every morning she'd wake up early to read her Bible, pray, and journal. As the sun rose, she treasured this precious quiet time with God. Eventually her two-year-old would wake and wander out to find Julie, and the two would cuddle on the couch for a while. What a great way to start the day!

But life happens, doesn't it? Eventually the children were older, they were in school, and Julie was back at work. Things were suddenly crazier than they'd ever been, and Julie's quiet time became a thing of the past. One Sunday morning she picked up her Bible, read a few passages, and tried to pray, but it just didn't seem to be working. She felt disconnected and unmotivated. And although she kept trying to rekindle her romance with God, the spark just never seemed to catch.

It's not unusual for us to get busy and neglect our spiritual lives. When that happens, it can be extremely difficult to reawaken that side of ourselves. If you find yourself in some kind of spiritual desert, here are a few things to think about:

- Your spiritual life is a relationship with Jesus. You can sometimes fall into the trap of thinking your spiritual life should be sort of magical and full of blessings, insights, and miracles, but that's not true. Like any relationship, it doesn't "just happen"; you have to maintain it. When you don't and it goes dry, there will be some catch-up work to do. This is normal, and it happens to all of us.

- When you feel disengaged from God, it's often a symptom of a general disconnect in your life. Have you gotten so busy that you're disconnecting from other people as well? Is there some other issue going on that's making you want to detach from your feelings? What's going on between you and God is probably not limited to your spiritual life. Begin to explore what else is going on.

+ How you interact with God can be related to how you relate to your parents, particularly your earthly father. Is there something about your relationship with your dad that you're projecting onto God?

+ Sometimes we separate from God as a result of overall feelings of worthlessness or failure. Explore if you are going through something like this. Dealing with that issue can help reawaken your spiritual vitality.

+ Knowingly living with some kind of repetitive or unconfessed sin also separates you from God. The guilt and shame keep you from wanting to be in His presence. Is there a sin issue you need to deal with to get right with God again?

+ Occasionally we simply have no identifiable reason for being in a dry place, but we just feel stuck in a rut. Maybe you need to shake things up a bit. Try visiting a different church, or several over the next few weeks. Spend an hour at a bookstore, searching for a devotional that speaks to you. Go for a "walk with God" on your lunch hour rather than trying to carve out time in the early morning.

## SPIRITUAL SECRETS
### *If You Are in a Spiritual Desert*

There are all sorts of ways to rejuvenate your relationship with God, and many books provide answers. I can't go into all the possibilities here, but I want to bring your attention to something simple that might help. It's easy to think that if you're having trouble praying or are not interested in reading Scripture, that you need to try harder. That's usually not the case. I'd like you to think instead about *doing something different.*

Each of us has something we enjoy doing or experiencing that somehow feeds our soul. It's usually something for which we don't have time. My friend Lynne loves to go hiking with her dog on local mountain trails. It gives her a chance to enjoy God's creation and appreciate the beauty of His handiwork. Another friend is into gardening, finding that having her hands in the dirt feels more spiritual than anything else. Someone else spends time knitting whenever possible, cherishing the way it seems to calm her spirit. Many women integrate praise and worship music into their day, while driving or exercising or even while cleaning house. I've found that for me, taking an art class helps me feel the most alive and in touch with myself and God. Something about working on a painting takes me out of my day-to-day and into a sacred place where God and I exist together.

Is there something you can do—something that doesn't necessarily appear spiritual on the surface—that makes you feel alive? Is it possible for you to add that one activity into your schedule? If not, you may want to look at your calendar and find a time when it *will* be possible—and write it down. Reading books, attending Bible study, going to church—those are all good things. But if you're in the spiritual dark place, maybe you need to put less focus on all the normal things and find a back door into your spirit. Ask God to meet you there, and watch what happens.

## Think About It
*If You Are Spiritually Disconnected from Your Husband*

If your husband isn't the perfect Christian man you want him to be, you might be stuck in the "if only" trap. *If only my husband were a Christian, or a better one, we could really be happy together! If only he would be a spiritual leader in our household, I could relax, and our family would be "right" in God's eyes.* Unfortunately, we can't live by if-onlys but must deal with reality. Here are some thoughts to lead you in a productive direction:

- I've noticed that the church culture tends to give us unrealistic expectations for what a family *should* be or how a man *should* behave. The reality is that most men are uncomfortable being "out there" with their spiritual experience. They're more private and may not enjoy talking about it. Even if your husband is a strong believer, he may not be a leader type but more of a behind-the-scenes guy. You cannot make your husband into someone he's not. Think about what standards you are using to judge him. Do you need to redefine your idea of *good Christian* or *spiritual leader*?

- Rather than focus on specific behaviors you wish to see in your husband, ask yourself if he exhibits any attributes of godliness without necessarily ever talking about God. Focus on his strengths—the ways that he shows his love for you and the family, the ways he supports or accepts your own approach to church and spirituality. Reframe your spiritual disconnect with your husband so it's no longer a point of friction or a way for you to judge him, simply a way that you two are different from each other.

- Remember that men feel loved when they are respected. Show your respect for him by refusing to judge or belittle him about his spiritual place in life. Instead, focus on simply having nonthreatening conversations with him. Let him know your thoughts on something spiritual—*not* about him—and ask him what he thinks. Get away from the mind-set that because he's not the same as you, he's wrong.

- Women can easily make their husbands feel inadequate and lacking in the spiritual department. Do you sense that your husband feels like a failure in this area? You can contribute to this by being too vocal or pushy about your expectations for him. Unfortunately, the more you try to talk with him about it, the more he retreats. Sometimes the best approach is to completely back off. Simply live your life and handle your relationship with God and spiritual pursuits on your own, while concentrating on loving your husband without expecting him to be someone else. If there comes a time when you feel comfortable discussing this with him, never focus on his performance or his spiritual life. Talk to him about yours, asking his thoughts and opinions. If and when he ever feels like discussing his own spiritual life, he will tell you about it.

- Remember that God works in everyone differently. People have growth spurts at different times. Allow your husband his own path. As author Patricia Raybon put it, "The job of winning souls is the work of the Holy Spirit, not the work of an arguing wife. A praying woman will win a man to Jesus faster than an arguing woman ever will."[1]

## Spiritual Secrets
### *If You Are Spiritually Disconnected from Your Husband*

If you're like most women who are dissatisfied with their husbands' spiritual positions, you may be in the habit of praying for him—specifically, that God would *change him* into what you want him to be! I'd like to suggest that you change the focus of your prayers.

First, begin praying more for yourself. Ask God to soften your heart toward your husband and to teach you how to love and accept him unconditionally. Ask God to show you how to use your gifts—wisdom, compassion, understanding—to more effectively relate to your husband.

Next, make sure you are praying for your husband, that God would work in him according to God's desire, not your own. Ask for the grace to let go of your expectations for your husband and to continue praying for God's will in his life.

If your husband seems interested, I recommend you consider some kind of Bible study or small group for couples. This is a way you both can be in the same place and involved in the same biblical discussions, even though you are in very different places spiritually. Most likely, things will be discussed that you've never talked about at home, and it just might open up the possibility for that kind of discussion in private. If he's not enthused about the couples' study idea, gently suggest a men's group. Some kind of involvement with other believers is an important step in spiritual maturity. However, if none of these appeals to him, don't push it. Let him be who he is.

Beyond prayer and small groups, you can concentrate on truly loving your husband in a nonjudgmental way. Set a quiet example for him, letting the fruit of the Spirit shine through as you continue on your own faith walk. Let go of any need to be "holier than thou," and resist the urge to flaunt your piousness or show off your incredible Bible knowledge. Remember that your husband's salvation and his faith journey are between him and God—however difficult, you might be left out of the equation. This is okay. Let it be.

## FROM SECRETS TO SOLUTIONS

If you're experiencing a spiritual disconnect—from yourself, from your husband, or from God—then keeping it a secret is only going to lead to further disconnect. If your goal is greater connection, the first step is bringing your secret into your own consciousness, then perhaps bringing it in front of someone else who can help you with it.

*Be honest with yourself.* Why are you keeping the secret of your spiritual issues? Is it because you're afraid of what people will think? Do you feel as though you're the only one, or are you ashamed? Explore if there's a secret underneath that you've been keeping hidden from yourself. Maybe it's a sin issue that's separating you from God. Maybe it's a desperate fear for your husband's eternal soul. Whatever the hidden secret is, try to root it out.

*Be honest with God.* Pray about the results of this soul-searching.

Ask God to reveal anything that you haven't become aware of yet. Use language that's *real*, even if it feels strange. *God, I haven't been in touch with You lately, I don't know why, but I'm just not into this right now!* Lay out for God everything that you can identify about your struggles and fears in this area. Ask God to show you the next steps.

*Be honest with someone else.* You may decide to open up in your small group, or perhaps with a Christian friend. Maybe there is a counseling pastor at your church who can help. The key is to choose someone in your life, someone who is *safe*, and open up about this struggle. Ask a friend to join you in a spiritual growth stretch—going on a silent retreat or seeking out someone who does spiritual direction. I can practically guarantee you'll find out you're not alone, and hopefully you will even gain some perspective on your situation and some ideas for moving forward.

## PRAYING SCRIPTURE FOR YOUR SECRET

Pray John 4:14.

Lord, I have been experiencing troubles in my spiritual life, but You said, "Whoever drinks the water I give him will never thirst. Indeed, the water I give him will become in him a spring of water welling up to eternal life." I ask You, Lord, to fill me up with Your living water—Yourself—and never let me stray from my walk with You. Amen.

## RECOMMENDED RESOURCES

### FOR SPIRITUAL DRYNESS
*Blue Like Jazz: Nonreligious Thoughts on Christian Spirituality* by Donald Miller
*How People Grow* by Henry Cloud and John Townsend
*New Life Every Day Devotional* (Vol. 4) by Steve Arterburn
*Reframe Your Life: Transforming Your Pain into Purpose* by Stephen Arterburn

*The Ragamuffin Gospel: Good News for the Bedraggled, Beat Up, and Burnt Out* by Brennan Manning
*The Secret Things of God* by Henry Cloud
*The 3:16 Promise: He Loves. He Gives. We Believe. We Live* by Max Lucado
*12 "Christian" Beliefs that Can Drive You Crazy* by Henry Cloud and John Townsend

## FOR SPIRITUALLY UNEQUAL MARRIAGE
*Beloved Unbeliever* by Jo Kennedy
*How to Be the Happy Wife of an Unsaved Husband* by Linda Davis
*Surviving a Spiritual Mismatch in Marriage* by Lee Strobel
*When He Doesn't Believe: Help and Encouragement for Women Who Feel Alone in Their Faith* by Nancy Kennedy

# Chapter 13

# I Suffer from Depression

I guess I would say my biggest secret would be my depression. I think there is this stigma that if someone is feeling depressed for a long time, they are either being needy or they just need to get over it.

✦ ✦ ✦

Lately I have realized how shut down emotionally I am. I'm trying to hold on and find a reason to care. I feel emotionally flatlined. I just want to be held and to cry and to allow the little girl in me to cry.

I once had a neighbor who was a vivacious, lovely woman with an active social life. She always seemed to be surrounded by friends, throwing parties, and enjoying herself. But she went through a season in which she suffered a couple of difficult losses within a short period of time, and I noticed her habits suddenly changed. There were no more parties. Few friends coming and going. And it seemed that she never went out anymore—her drapes remained closed, and I rarely saw her except when she left the house for work. When I tried to reach out to her, she first brushed me off, telling me she was sick with the flu, a sinus infection, or allergies. Eventually I was able to talk to her, and after hearing about the things that had been happening in her life, I gently asked her if she'd considered seeking treatment for depression.

Like most people who are depressed, she could barely admit it, let alone seek treatment for it. I was able to reassure her that her pain was legitimate, that it didn't have to be purely physical to be taken seriously. She reluctantly allowed me to point her in the direction toward help. After a few months I noticed her "old self" returning, and she appeared to be enjoying life much like before.

Depression is one of the most common difficulties people deal with in life, yet a small percentage of those who suffer actually seek treatment. The first thing I want you to realize about depression is that, left untreated, it usually gets worse, not better. The second thing I'll tell you is that depression is not a life sentence. With the proper help and a plan for wellness, you do *not* have to suffer forever.

## Unlocking the Secret

Everyone knows what it's like to feel down or blue. We all have disappointments, setbacks, and heartbreaks. Being *bummed out* in response to our circumstances is normal, and usually short-lived. Soon we pick ourselves up and resume life, perhaps the worse for wear but still functioning.

Depression, on the other hand, is debilitating to some degree. It infiltrates every aspect of our being—emotional, physical, mental, and spiritual. It keeps us from doing things and living life in the way that we normally do. It can be a chronic low-grade depression (known as dysthymic disorder) that prevents us from fully enjoying the high moments and makes all of our functions just a little more difficult. We have trouble concentrating well, sleeping soundly, relating to others, staying organized, and simply feeling on top of our lives. Or it can be a major depression in which we literally cannot get out of bed. And there are countless variations in between.

If you are depressed, you may be thinking you should get some help, but you just don't have the energy. That's the ironic thing about depression. You need all your strength to deal with it and try to fight it, but you feel you have no strength at all. You know you need to do something, but you simply can't muster up the energy to do anything. If you're in this place, please just do one thing: keep reading to the end of this chapter; then use our listed resources to try to do one more thing.

## KEEPING THE SECRET

With the pervasiveness of depression in our society, it's almost surprising how many still suffer in silence. There is so much help available. Yet there is also a stigma attached to depression. People tend to think of it as a character problem—as if the depressed person is simply "not trying hard enough," or she's whiny or self-absorbed. If you're depressed, you may be telling yourself you just need to *snap out of it.*

But snap-out-of-it therapy doesn't work. People who are depressed can't simply *will* themselves to be well. So they begin to feel guilty, wondering what they're doing wrong and why they can't seem to get it together. They feel ashamed of their feelings and the way they can't always control their behavior. They look around them and see all the people with smiles on their faces, living life as usual, and they can't help but think, *What's wrong with me that I can't seem to enjoy life like everyone else?* They feel alone.

One of the biggest problems with depression is that it makes you want to isolate yourself from others. You go inward and stop relating as you used to. You may feel as though you want to crawl in a hole, or put the covers over your head and stay that way for a week. But the isolation increases the depression. Keeping it to yourself—like all the other secrets in this book—is not the answer.

## THINK ABOUT IT

My secret is that my smile hides my depression.

+ + +

I am scared I will continue to wish for suicide the rest of my life.

+ + +

I don't want to be here anymore.

+ + +

I am committing suicide, but no one will know because I'm doing it slowly by eating too much and being obese.

+ + +

I want to kill myself, but I never would.

These words from women writing on our Secrets Blog are heartbreaking, but I've included them to show you that you are not alone; and further, that suffering in silence can make the depression worsen until you are actually at risk of suicide. I want to help you avoid that place. (If you are having thoughts of suicide, please call 1-800-New Life. There are people ready and waiting to help you right now.)

I'm going to tell you about symptoms, causes, and types of

depression, and the typical treatments offered. But this is only a brief overview. I encourage you to use the resources listed at the end of this chapter to find further information and determine the kind of help that would be best for you.

It's important to recognize the symptoms of depression so that you can identify it in yourself or someone else. The most obvious one is feeling blue or sad most every day, although this isn't always the biggest symptom. You may simply feel that you don't enjoy things as you used to. You may gain or lose weight unnaturally fast; you may either have insomnia or sleep too much as a way of avoiding life. You may have difficulty getting going at the start of the day, overwhelmed by dread for what lies ahead. Fatigue and loss of energy are common, as are feelings of helplessness or worthlessness. Lack of ability to think well or concentrate may plague you. You may feel disorganized and not able to stay on top of your schedule and responsibilities. Obviously, we all experience some of these circumstances occasionally. But clinical depression means that you have several of them at the same time for an extended period of time.

Why do people get depressed? Some of the causes are intuitively obvious. People are often emotionally incapacitated following a major calamity or loss. The death of a loved one, serious illness, divorce, and even relocation are all common precipitators of depression. Even happy events that cause life changes, such as marriage or the birth of a baby, can leave someone depressed in the aftermath.

But depression doesn't have to stem from a single catastrophe or event. Some people have a genetic predisposition for depression. Others have a chemical imbalance of the neurotransmitters in the brain. There are health issues such as hormonal imbalances or bodily changes due to pregnancy and menopause, and countless other physical possibilities. Some people become depressed when the smaller stressors of life add up and become too overwhelming to handle. Many women who are the victims of long-term mistreatment, verbal abuse, and disrespect become depressed. There is a feeling of hopelessness in being personally rejected and devalued repeatedly over time. The loss of your health or the loss of a dream or hoped-for future can cause depression too.

While I'm not going to go into an exhaustive list of the various mood disorders or their diagnostic criteria here, I want to point out that the term *depression* can include general symptoms overlapping into a wide variety of disorders, or a specific disorder itself. Therefore, you can be struggling with myriad difficulties and have depressive symptoms. Or like an umbrella, depression covers you and depresses your specific feelings, causing a general cloudiness (hence the black cloud effect). A major depressive disorder is a very visible, more extreme condition characterized by severely impaired functioning, such as not being able to get out of bed, withdrawal, all-or-nothing thinking, limited capacity to see a way out, and/or suicidal fantasies. A dysthymic disorder is more low-grade and long-term (at least two years), and it can be harder to spot because it comes on gradually and isn't as dramatically noticeable. It can be brought on by cumulative trauma, which is not related to any one event but stems from repetitive misattunements originating with primary caregivers and continuing with significant others throughout life.

Many Christians feel guilty for feeling depressed when they don't have some identifiable event to point to. Some people have seasonal affective disorder, which is a pattern of depression affected by the seasons, the weather, and the amount of sunlight in the environment. Bipolar disorder (and its variations) is a kind of two-faceted disorder that swings back and forth on a continuum between periods of a mood that appears "up," (high in energy, manic, expansive flights of ideas) to periods of being sad, blue, depressed, or suicidal. There are other categories and variations; the important thing to understand is that the term *depression* can show itself in many different ways.

Usually the most effective treatment for depression is a combination of psychotherapy and antidepressant medication. Therapy provides a safe place to bring all the issues, and it provides some comfort and soothing. It's kind of like a holding environment for all the things that are getting you down. Since depression makes you feel really alone, therapy is a way to know there's someone who understands and can really hear your pain. Along with psychotherapy, anti-depressant medication can be a powerful tool for helping you get through a difficult season of life and resume normal functioning. The point is not to mask the pain but to lift the bottom enough with medication so that you have the strength and ability to begin honestly dealing with the problems that caused your depression.

Getting involved with groups of people can be tremendously helpful. There are support groups, recovery groups, even Bible study groups or prayer groups. You want to try to stop isolating yourself, and join others with whom you can identify and who can lend you support.

As you are thinking about what kind of treatment to seek or who to call, realize there are things you can do for yourself. It may be difficult, but the point is to take small steps. Just do one thing at a time. Allow yourself to be depressed, realizing there is no shame in it. Accept the feelings—without surrendering to them. Getting out of depression is often like a battle. You have to fight it by taking one small step at a time in some direction, any direction. Depending on where you are in your level of functioning, you might focus on simply getting out of bed and showering, or you may make a phone call to discuss talking to a counselor. Maybe you can't force yourself to get out to the supermarket, but can you walk around the block? With depression, the recovery process is all about little movements that can add up to a big difference.

Most people who are depressed believe they're always going to be that way. It's one of the hallmarks of depression—the inability to see beyond it. But I've seen a lot of people who have been depressed, to the point of being suicidal, work through it and come out the other side. It takes a serious commitment to treatment and a sincere desire to get better. Once you get treatment and get a good handle on your issues and ways to approach them in a healthy way, you can find your life rejuvenated. If you have a lifelong pattern of depression, you might fall back into it occasionally during difficult times. But it usually won't be as deep or long lasting.

## Spiritual Secrets

Anna was a forty-one-year-old woman who had reached rock bottom. In a matter of a few months, she'd strayed far from the Lord and become tangled in sin; she'd lost her dream job, most of her friends, her reputation, and possibly her career; her marriage was in shambles, and divorce papers were being drawn; and because of all this, financial devastation loomed. Anna found herself sleeping in her car in the parking lot of a supermarket in her upper-middle-class neighborhood, praying for God to take her life.

But God had other plans. He sent a new friend, seemingly out of nowhere, who offered Anna healthy food, a warm bed, and a listening ear. This godly woman picked Anna up, dusted her off, and showed her the love of Jesus simply by being there. Anna remembers this as a turning point in her emotional journey.

"I remained depressed for several months after that," she said, "but after that rock-bottom moment and being rescued, the misery began to ease in tiny increments, day by day. It was a lot of work, getting out of the depression. But it's been three years, and I honestly can't believe how full of joy my life is now."

Anna's journey from deep depression to a healthy, contented life included traditional psychotherapy; a year of antidepressant medication; a spiritual path of confession, deep repentance, and restoration; and focus on the basics of physical health: good food, enough sleep, plenty of exercise. Like many Christians, Anna was reluctant to take medication, believing it wasn't spiritual or somehow meant she didn't have enough faith. But soon she realized her depression was so deep it was keeping her from relating to God. She couldn't pray, and she couldn't read the Bible. She was barely able to function physically or emotionally. She needed help in lifting the worst of the debilitating despair so that she would have the emotional and physical resources to begin rebuilding her life. "Antidepressants allowed me to finally start thinking clearly so that I could begin to get my life back on track. I honestly don't know where I'd be if I hadn't taken them," Anna related.

Depression is seen in several places in the Bible. David wrote of despair and hopelessness repeatedly in the Psalms. In Romans 7:18, we find Paul struggling with depression about his inability to "do what is good." In 1 Kings 19, the prophet Elijah became depressed and prayed that he might die (v. 4). I love how God ministered to Elijah in his hopelessness. First, God addressed Elijah's physical needs. He had Elijah sleep for a long time, and then He gave Elijah food and water, saying, "Get up and eat, for the journey is too much for you" (v. 7). God knew that Elijah's path ahead would be tough (he was about to travel forty days and nights on foot through the desert), and God knows that *your* journey out of depression will be tough too. Remember to start with the basics of physical survival— rest, food, exercise, and medication if necessary.

God also gave Elijah encouragement as well as a new friend, Elisha, who was to be Elijah's attendant and would eventually be his successor. God knows how important it is that we do not try to travel this path alone. Sure, we have God Himself, but we need other people too. Don't keep the secret of your depression. Like Elijah, you need an attendant, someone to encourage you and minister to you. The next section will give you some ideas about how to find this person.

Above all, please remember that depression isn't anything new— not to God and not among humans. There are remedies as old as mankind and other treatments that are brand-new. God doesn't want you to suffer in desolation forever. He wants you to grab onto Him and His love and all of the resources He makes available, and let Him pull you out.

## From Secrets to Solutions

The essential thing to know about the secret of depression is that the solution lies in refusing to keep it secret any longer. When depression remains hidden, it festers and gets worse. It is only when it is brought to light that it can be treated and you can find your way back to life.

*Be honest with yourself.* It's crucial for you to candidly admit to yourself that you are—or think you might be—suffering from depression. Then stop rationalizing it. Don't allow yourself to think, *It'll go away soon* or *I can't tell anybody—I just need to get my act together.* Admit to yourself that you are depressed and that you need to talk with someone about it.

*Be honest with God.* As we've discussed, you are not the first person to cry out to God that you're depressed! Your state of mind could make it difficult to pray, but you don't have to think of it as prayer. Just talk to God as you would to your closest friend or confidante. Tell Him how you feel. Let Him know if you are confused or angry or hopeless. Then tell Him you need His help! Ask Him to guide you out of this darkness and out into the light. Don't feel as though you need to be poetic or speak in flowery language. Just lay it out there.

*Be honest with a therapist, psychologist, or other trained professional.* This is the most important step for clinical depression. Rarely will you find a solution without some assistance from those who know what they're doing. You can ask at your church, or you can call 1-800-New-Life and ask for a referral to a local Christian counselor. You can check with your own insurance company or medical group and find a psychologist. There are numerous ways to avail yourself of the expertise that's out there. Please find a way. Make the call!

Who else in your life can you talk with about your depression so that you will not feel so alone? Is there a friend you can trust? Think about other ways you might open up. There are all kinds of recovery groups available. It is helpful to maximize your resources and find people who truly understand and won't just try to convince you out of your feelings. Especially if you are a long-time sufferer, it is important to seek help from others outside of your family. Family members often feel powerless, frustrated, and angry toward the one who suffers because it directly affects them. So in this instance your husband, kids, or siblings may be too close to fully understand, and they may have lost their compassion under the weight of your depression. Don't leave them out of the loop, but let them know that you are going to do something proactive to help yourself. They may be relieved and come alongside you instead of resenting your previous passive state.

The most important thing I want you to remember is that you may be struggling, but you are not alone. Many people have walked this road before you and are walking it now. People have walked through the deepest depression and come out the other side. There is hope—you don't have to live in this hopelessness for a lifetime. There are ways out.

Please, as soon as possible, take the next step. Do just one thing toward finding a way out. Buy a book. Log on to a Web site. Make a phone call. Do one thing. And then, do the next.

## Praying Scripture for Your Secret

Pray Psalm 142:1–3, 6–7.

> I cry aloud to You, Lord; I lift up my voice to You for mercy. I pour out my complaint before You; before You I tell my trouble. When my spirit grows faint within me, it is You who know my way. Listen to my cry, for I am in desperate need. Set me free from the prison of my depression, that I may praise Your name. Amen.

## Recommended Resources

New Life—www.newlife.com
  1-800-New-Life (1-800-639-5433)
Focus on the Family
  1-800-A-Family (1-800-232-6459)
New Hope Counseling Center
  1-714-New-Hope (1-714-639-4673)

Suicide Hotline
   1-800-SUICIDE (1-800-784-2433)

BOOKS
*Breaking Free from Depression* by Linda Mintle
*Depression: A Stubborn Darkness—Light for the Path* by Edward T.
   Welch
*Happiness Is a Choice: The Symptoms, Causes, and Cures of
   Depression* by Frank Minirth and Paul Meier
*Healing Is a Choice Devotional* by Steve Arterburn
*I've Got the Blues: God's Plan for Beating Depression* by Mike
   Marino
*New Light on Depression: Help, Hope, and Answers for the Depressed
   and Those Who Love Them* by David B. Biebel and Harold
   George Koenig
*What to Do When You Don't Know What to Do: Discouragement and
   Depression* by Henry Cloud and John Townsend
*When Saints Sing the Blues: Understanding Depression Through the
   Lives of Job, Naomi, Paul, and Others* by Brenda Poinsett

*Part Five*

SECRETS ABOUT
OUR SENSE OF SELF

# Chapter 14

# I Feel Invisible
# or Inadequate

I am in my thirties, and I am realizing that I do not even know who I really am, what I want, or what would make me happy. I do not know how to get to my real self.

✦ ✦ ✦

I feel completely insecure about myself at times, while pretending to the world that I have it all together.

✦ ✦ ✦

I feel like nobody. Outside I put on a smile, but I am lonely. I long to connect with people but do not know where to begin.

✦ ✦ ✦

My secret is that I am inadequate and never as good at anything as everyone else. I just feel I can never compare to women around me, and I am so insecure and have such low self-esteem. I know I'm too critical of myself, but I cannot help it!

Mary is a young woman, married with two children, living a stable middle-class life. But she grew up in a poor environment, and her mother was illiterate, ashamed, and unhappy; consequently, Mary's growing-up years were filled with a bombardment of negative messages about herself: "You can't do that," and "Who do you think you are?" As an adult, Mary is besieged by constant feelings that she is not good enough, and she often doesn't feel seen or heard by her own family. Mary realizes she has lost her sense of self or never fully developed it, and she wants to find it, but hasn't a clue where to start looking.

---

## Unlocking the Secret

Right now, millions of women are walking around feeling that they don't matter, or that they don't know who they are, or that they are simply *not good enough*. Can you relate to this? If so, you're probably feeling helpless along with your already difficult feelings of inadequacy. You don't know *why* you feel this way, and you have no idea where to begin to fix it. There are ways to uncover how you got here, and more importantly, there is a path to a new, more confident, more vibrant *you*.

This feeling of being inadequate or invisible takes various forms. Many women start their adult lives already beaten down by negative family relationship patterns or terrible experiences in school. When you're told or have experienced over and over that you don't matter, or if you have drawn the conclusion that you're not important enough to be anyone's number one priority, eventually you believe those messages. If you had a hard time fitting in as a teen—and let's face it, the world of middle school and high school can be brutal—then maybe you emerged feeling that you don't "fit in" in life, either. This doesn't imply that you were a total outcast; it's about your internal experience, especially in the midst of others. These situations lead you to lose your sense of self, or neglect to develop one in the first place. You become passive and unable to voice your thoughts or opinions. You may not even know what your own opinions are.

As you move into young adulthood with these feelings, a time when you are making some of your biggest life decisions, it can be very overwhelming. You may fall into choices about schooling, career interests, and whether to marry based on stronger voices around you, and later you wonder how you got where you are. Instead of individuating, you gave up *you* for the desires and wants of others who you thought you knew better.

Have you ever had an experience of sitting in a group of people who are all talking and expressing themselves, and you find yourself nodding enthusiastically at everyone else's comments but have nothing to add of your own? Perhaps you're thinking, as each person speaks, *Yes! I agree with that!* But you are unable to form an opinion that is strictly your own. This is a sign that you're lacking or have an underdeveloped sense of self.

Some women start off adulthood with a strong awareness of who they are separate from others, but in the daily grind of motherhood, wifehood, workhood, and catering to everyone else's needs, they one day wake up and realize they don't know who they are anymore. Women's magazines are full of admonitions to schedule some "me time" into your life, and this is a good idea. But I think the problem is not so much that we don't have the *time*—we have actually lost the *me*. You've spent so many years letting yourself be defined by the needs of others that you've become like the tail of a kite—constantly being whipped around but never going anywhere on your own. You start second-guessing yourself and find that you're reluctant to give your opinion. You wonder: *Where did I go? What happened to the self-confident woman I used to be?*

All of this leads to big self-image problems, and it's made worse by our media culture that bombards us with unrealistic images of perfection. We are already too dependent on others in trying to define ourselves, so when we look at media portrayals of role models, all we get is a rude slap in the face: *You will never be this beautiful—skinny—smart—successful—perfect.* We easily can get in the habit of seeing ourselves as never measuring up, never being good enough to meet some arbitrary standard. We feel like complete failures, and it can lead to a perception of ourselves as being worthless.

You look around, and even your girlfriends or the members of your small group seem to have it all together. Of course, when they look at you, they think *you* have it all together too. That's because it's the image most of us present to the world. And that leads us to yet another variation of the I-am-inadequate problem, which is "I feel like a fraud." When we present one image to the world ("I'm doing great") but feel differently inside ("I am a mess"), we know we are being incongruent. There's a disconnect between our insides and our outsides. As one woman wrote on the Secrets Blog, "I am afraid someone will find out that I am a fake."

All of these patterns of thought and feeling—whether you call it insecurity, inadequacy, invisibility, being a fraud—all of them come down to a failure to fully *own ourselves.* That's just a fancy way of saying we're in the habit of looking to others for a sense of who we are and to tell us we are okay, and we've lost touch with the real women God intended us to be.

## Keeping the Secret

It's kind of a no-brainer that we would keep these feelings a secret. Almost every woman has some kind of issue with feeling invisible, inadequate, or like a fraud or failure. And yet we all somehow believe "nobody else feels this" or at least we think there are only a few women who might know how we feel. Let me just clear up that misconception right now: it's virtually all of us!

Somehow the culture leads you to believe there's something out there that's attainable—some level of perfection or feeling that you've *arrived*—and you just haven't figured it out yet. If you could just get a handle on it, then you could pull it together and "be all that," right? Like most of us, you're falling into the trap of comparing your insides to everyone else's outsides.

You're not alone. Most of us do it constantly. We project the *good* onto others and the *bad* onto ourselves. We *know* ourselves—we're well aware of our weaknesses and flaws. But we don't know what's going on inside other women. We forget that they're feeling as flawed as we are. So we keep these feelings to ourselves, and that's a big mistake. The moment you begin opening up about your insecurities is the moment you'll start hearing other women say, "Me too."

Deep down we all want to feel *heard*—that someone is willing to listen to what we have to say; *seen*—that we are known and understood at a heart level; and *valued*—that we are loved and appreciated for who we truly are.

## Think About It

Most of us walk around with what I call an *internal parent*, chattering nonstop inside our brains. This isn't necessarily the voice of our *real* parent but a compilation of all the negative messages we've ever heard about ourselves. That grating little voice is constantly running, telling us how we're not good enough, how nobody understands us, how nobody hears or sees us or cares about us. The good news is that there are some solid strategies you can use to break the cycle—to stop listening to that irritating refrain and start being more of who you were made to be.

The first thing to do is identify that there's a problem. Hopefully from reading this chapter so far, you've already begun to recognize your own tendencies toward feeling inadequate or invisible. You might want to take some time and journal about this. What are the disapproving messages you hear in your head? How long has this been going on?

The next step would be to take a risk and tell someone about it (see "From Secrets to Solutions" later in this chapter). If you already don't feel heard or seen, and you're not used to speaking up, then this is going to be a big step of faith. Choose someone you believe is safe and trustworthy, and start by telling her just a tiny bit of your struggle. As time goes on and you receive feedback, affirmation, and the comfort of not being alone, you may want to slowly talk about more of your feelings with this person.

If you're in a Bible study or women's group that has been together long enough to have built a sense of trust, you might want to bring it up there. You'll need to gauge your group's readiness for this discussion based on the level of depth that's already occurring. Are people getting real with their thoughts and feelings? Does it feel safe (even though it might not exactly be comfortable)? If so, you can begin with a simple statement, something like, "I've wanted to speak up in this group, and it's been hard for me. I think it's because for some reason, I have lost my sense of self, and I feel inadequate around others. I've been thinking about this lately, and this is the first time I've actually said it out loud." Many times I've seen an admission such as this become a life-changing moment for a woman who, for the first time, discovers that others have felt the same way she does.

After this, it's time to start taking some practical steps to begin developing a more solid sense of yourself. Begin asking yourself a few questions, What do I think about that? What do I feel? What is my opinion? What do I like and dislike? Pick up the newspaper, read a column, and then take a few moments to sit with it, formulating a response. You might find it difficult at first if you're in the habit of ignoring or invalidating your own thoughts and feelings. It can be uncomfortable. But it's a necessary step in becoming who you are. If you go to a movie with friends, pay attention to your honest responses, and practice speaking them out loud (*after* the movie, of course). If you're in Bible study, be alert to your own responses to the material rather than simply listening to everyone else's. Then practice talking about them.

I've seen plenty of moms who can no longer readily identify foods they truly like, the music that speaks to their souls, or the types of movies they sincerely enjoy. When asked their favorites, they may even respond by listing the choices of family members and never mention their own. They've been focused for so long on the preferences of their husband and children that they've ceased to even realize they might have their own likes and dislikes. It's crucial that you begin to rediscover yourself in these small, practical ways.

Shelly is a midforties wife and mom who got frustrated after a decade of dinners and television shows her family enjoyed—which hardly ever coincided with her own favorites. She made a list of the things she missed, such as herbal teas and exotic cheeses, taped some TV programs she wanted to try out, and began a new tradition. Whenever possible, a little while before dinner (or even while preparing it), she would take a *mom break* and enjoy her chamomile tea or brie and crackers and watch one of her taped shows. At other times she would read a devotional or a good book. It sounds simple, but this little ritual began connecting her to the idea that she was a whole person, separate from her family, and that she was allowed her own tastes, opinions, and preferences. She also found it helped her to relax and enjoy the rest of the evening, now that she'd had some time and space to *be herself*.

Some women have been so beaten down and hard on themselves that even the physical quality of their voice is diminished. Do you speak softly, almost in a whisper, or in a high-pitched squeak? If so, it's time for some basic assertion training. Practice speaking in a full, assertive voice, no matter where you are.

If you're a mom and often hear only your exasperated or yelling kind of voice, you might not feel this applies to you. If you have no trouble marching up to a supermarket clerk and loudly complaining about the poor quality of the bananas, you might think you have a strong enough sense of yourself, thank you very much. But ask yourself whether your loud voice is coming from a place of quiet strength or assertiveness or even confidence . . . or whether it might be coming from a deeper place of inadequacy, and it's your way of overcompensating. Just consider all the angles.

You've heard the phrase *act as if*. Sometimes the best way to begin developing confidence in yourself is to act as if you are confident. Speak in a way that says, "I deserve to be heard!" This is so important because you'll soon find that when you change your approach to others, the responses you get will also change. When you are in the habit of being timid or acting as if you're not really worth anyone's time, others will treat you that way. If you go the opposite direction and try to steamroll your way through situations, you won't be treated kindly. But if you appear confident and worthy, people will treat you with respect. This is a crucial part of developing your sense of self—seeing a new image of you reflected back from other people.

Repetition is a vital part of this process as well. You'll need to repeat these new behaviors as often as you can, and keep doing them over and over. Whenever you're interacting with people, you'll need to be alert and aware, paying attention to how you speak and present yourself. Otherwise, you'll easily fall back into your old, I'm-not-good-enough patterns.

The problem is that when you *behave* as if you're inadequate, then people will treat you as if you're exactly that. They won't hear you or see you, just as you fear. If you want to change how others respond to you, your behavior will have to change first.

You may need to take steps to actively quiet those negative internal voices. Write down a list of positive things people have said about you in the past (think hard!). Tape them to your bathroom mirror, or carry them in your wallet. Then when you hear that old annoying rerun, tell it to stop, and replace it with some of the positives.

Here's another essential step for you to take: when someone

compliments you or says anything positive about you—*accept it*. Never again are you to downplay or reject any kudos sent your way. The best thing to do is say a simple thank-you even though you may be cringing when you do it (since you're so used to batting away anything positive). Remember, the other person is entitled to his or her opinion even if it is about you. So give that individual the respect of at least considering what he or she thinks. Then, as best you can, receive it. Accept it. Allow it to become part of who you are.

In your relationships, perhaps with your husband, your kids, or your boss, do you often feel tuned out or ignored? As though you don't really matter? Begin doing and saying things differently than you always have in the past. Women in this situation usually say things like, "I've tried everything to get his attention!" But in reality they've tried the same things, over and over. Try even saying what you always say to him, in the way you always say it, while looking in a mirror (maybe when no one is home), and see what you look like. Would you respond to you? I want you to examine your tone of voice, look at your body language, think carefully about your words, and do it differently. You can even use different settings or environments. Mix it up!

Another thing you can do in your quest to develop your sense of self is to start taking some time each week for something that makes you feel alive. Find something that brings you a feeling of quiet joy. There is nothing more wonderfully noticeable in others than aliveness. Take a walk through the woods or a local park. Draw a picture or play the piano or knit a scarf. Pull some weeds. Whatever it is that connects you with yourself, make the effort to add it into your schedule.

One last thing on developing a sense of yourself. Part of cultivating your own likes and dislikes is the ability to dress and style yourself in a way that's pleasing and comfortable to you. Have you been neglecting your physical appearance? Do you wear clothes from the eighties and cut your own hair? I find that people who feel invisible or unsatisfactory often "hide" themselves by appearing nondescript on the outside. Your physical self is an expression of who you are on the inside, so after you've been working on your sense of self, you'll want to begin allowing your outside to reflect who you really are. Again, ask yourself, What do I like? What colors appeal to me? What hairstyle would be most flattering to my face? Think about making a few small changes to your exterior that say to the world, "I care enough about myself to take care of myself. I'm worth caring about."

## SPIRITUAL SECRETS

As Christians and as women, we have a hard time with all of this focus on self, believing it automatically means we're being selfish or prideful. But that's not true. I believe it's imperative to fully be the women God created us to be, and anything less is to neglect the gift of life He gave us.

Jesus said, "Love your neighbor as yourself" (Matt. 19:19). Have you ever thought about the implication that you have to love yourself in order to love your neighbor? In this context, *love* is an action word, implying that you care for someone, that you minister to that person's needs. Loving yourself first means ministering to your own needs. If you constantly take care of others without taking care of yourself, soon you will be depleted and have nothing left to give. The well will be dry—and you can't get water from an empty well. You need to feed yourself, and of course, this means receiving spiritual food from prayer and Scripture and fellowshiping with other believers; but it also means taking the time to take care of yourself.

Jesus talked about the idea of denying yourself to follow Him (Matt. 16:24–25), and women often use this as a rationale for neglecting their own personal development. I'd like to point out that you cannot deny yourself if you don't really have a self to begin with. God wants you to be a whole, functioning, fully developed woman. He wants you to see yourself as He sees you—as beautiful, worthy, and eminently lovable. When you see yourself that way, then you are starting to see the person God created.

Deciding to be the whole woman God had in mind involves a day-by-day choice and a commitment to renewal. It's making a daily decision to love yourself in spite of yourself. You are a beautiful, purposefully created child of God. His creation is far from worthless, regardless of what anyone has ever told you. Decide today to take a different step, to do something differently, and become the person God sees when He looks at you.

## From Secrets to Solutions

The process of getting past invisibility or inadequacy involves giving up the secret of your unworthy feelings. Whatever other steps you decide to take, you must first let go of this secret burden that you carry all on your own.

*Be honest with yourself.* You can only begin becoming visible and worthy after you admit to yourself that this is an area you need to work on. Ask yourself some questions and explore exactly what situations make you feel inadequate and which people send you into an I'm-not-good-enough tailspin. Honestly assess how this has affected your relationships, your pursuit of your own goals and dreams, or your general level of contentedness.

*Be honest with God.* Pray about it, asking God to reveal the answers to any questions about yourself that confuse you. Let Him know exactly how invisible or unworthy you feel, and ask Him to begin showing you how He sees you.

*Be honest with a friend or counselor.* As I said above, you can talk to a friend, a study group, or anyone with whom it feels safe to share. If your negative self-image has drastically affected your life and the steps in this chapter seem impossible on your own, I highly recommend a psychologist or trained therapist. Sometimes it takes intense therapy to root out all the issues and set you on a more positive path.

## Praying Scripture for Your Secret

Pray Ephesians 3:16–20 (NLT).

> Father, Creator of everything in heaven and on earth, I
> pray that from Your glorious, unlimited resources You will
> empower me with inner strength through Your Spirit.
> Then Christ will make His home in my heart as I trust in
> You. My roots will grow down into Your love and keep me
> strong. And may I have the power to understand, as all
> God's people should, how wide, how long, how high, and
> how deep Your love is. May I experience the love of
> Christ, though it is too great to understand fully. Then I
> will be made complete with all the fullness of life and
> power that comes from You, God. Now all glory to God,
> who is able, through Your mighty power at work within
> us, to accomplish infinitely more than we might ask or
> think. Amen.

## Recommended Resources

*Being Perfect* by Anna Quindlen
*Boundaries: When to Say Yes, How to Say No, to Take Control of Your Life* by Henry Cloud and John Townsend
*Captivating: Unveiling the Mystery of a Woman's Soul* by John and Stasi Eldredge
*Hiding from Love: How to Change the Withdrawal Patterns that Isolate and Imprison You* by John Townsend
*Strong Women, Soft Hearts* by Paula Rinehart
*The Courage to Be Yourself: A Woman's Guide to Emotional Strength and Self-Esteem* by Sue Patton Thoele
*The Emotional Freedom Workbook* by Stephen Arterburn and Connie Neal
*The Invisible Woman: When Only God Sees* by Nicole Johnson

The Self-Confident Woman: Building a Strong Foundation for Healthy Relationships by Janet Congo
The Woman's Guide to Total Self-Esteem by Stephanie Dillon and Christina Benson
You Are What You Think by David Stoop

# Chapter 15

# I Obsess Over My Weight and Eating

It's foolish, I know, but no matter how great I look, I always feel I'm not thin enough, not in good enough shape, or not toned enough. Definitely a body image thing, but most of my friends admit to feeling the same way about themselves.

✦ ✦ ✦

I struggled with bulimia for years. Through prayer and being honest and accountable with someone, this cycle is being broken, and I am now eating more normally and my self-image is beginning to improve. I think I need professional help, but I've been afraid to get it.

✦ ✦ ✦

My secret is that I overeat so much that I've put us into serious credit card debt repeatedly, all of it spent on food. I had gastric bypass, but I am still enslaved to food. I feel hopeless about this.

Have you ever looked in the mirror and thought you were too fat (or too skinny)? Ever asked a girlfriend or husband, "Do these pants make me look fat?" Ever turned down your favorite dessert because you were "trying to be good"?

Of course you have. The fact that most American women obsess over their weight and eating is no secret at all. Sometimes it seems eating is our favorite national pastime, and trying to lose weight is a close second. Many women wrote to our Secrets Blog with their weight concerns and eating obsessions, sharing the pain of not only the problem but the secret. The most difficult thing to do is suffer alone, and in this chapter I hope to convince you to stop struggling in silence and come out into the light.

## Unlocking the Secret

Christy has always felt fat, ever since she was a child. As an adult she is significantly overweight, but when she looks back on childhood photos, she realizes she wasn't a chubby child. Did her image of herself as a fat person cause her to grow up and create that reality?

Ruth looks normal to anyone who comes in contact with her, but she is convinced she's fifteen pounds overweight. She struggles with those pounds as if they were a hundred, constantly dieting and then falling off her diet. She doesn't *look* as if she even needs to watch her weight, but still she obsesses over it. She has lost count of the number of diet books and fads she's tried, but those fifteen pounds remain. She is just as enslaved to food as if she were obese.

Jodi is another woman who doesn't appear overweight. People often compliment her on how good she looks. What nobody knows is that she's bulimic, bingeing and purging herself into a rapidly declining state of health. Food and weight are on her mind every day and night.

There are countless different ways women experience this secret obsession with weight and eating. Some are overweight; some are not. Some eat too much; others eat too much and then purge it; some compulsively control their food intake. But all are the same in one way: the unhealthy relationship to food keeps them from truly experiencing the fullness of life in the way God intended.

## Keeping the Secret

> I would have times when I would stuff food into my mouth, mindlessly, and I wasn't even hungry. I finally realized I was doing it because I was lonely, and/or bored, and/or depressed and that was how I coped. When I finally shared the secret with friends, a lot of its power went away.

The last thing you need is another book telling you how to lose weight! There are millions of words written on this topic already. And if you've been struggling for any length of time, you've probably read every book, tried every diet, and started and stopped so many fitness plans you've lost count. I trust that you've spent some time gathering knowledge about nutrition, exercise, healthy foods, and everything else related to reaching a healthy weight.

So I'm not going to talk much about those things, but I do want to deal with the aspect that's at issue right now—the fact that so many women are carrying this as a secret. It's completely understandable, considering how our society treats people who are overweight. Thinness is next to godliness—or above it in most cases—in our media-driven culture. In an era where it's un-PC to criticize practically anything, it's still acceptable to make fat jokes, act disgusted in the presence of an obese person, or send dirty looks when someone who's overweight walks into McDonald's and orders French fries. In this environment, it's easy to feel that you can't talk about your problem, can't even face it head-on in your own mind. The feelings of shame and self-loathing are overwhelming. One would think that since issues with weight and eating affect so many, they would be destigmatized, but they're not.

Nowadays, the media has figured out how to capitalize on our struggle with weight control. Several major television programs follow contestants through their journey to get in shape; celebrities are going public with their weight loss struggles; companies like Jenny Craig and Weight Watchers are highly visible. One of *People* magazine's most popular issues every year is the one with the before-and-after photos of people who have lost fifty or a hundred pounds or more. There are so many inspirational stories of people losing huge amounts of weight, it seems as if it should be motivating for those who struggle. But for many, these stories are having the opposite effect. They see what others are accomplishing, look at their own failures, and feel even worse. So the successes of others heap shame on top of shame, causing the problem to go underground and stay there.

Ironically, many women wrote about their secret binges, obsessions with food, and lifelong struggles with weight while being fully aware that their overweight bodies constantly advertise their problem to the world. The shame of this can cause you to retreat more and more into yourself so that while your body may be out there for all to see, your spirit is hiding, keeping your secrets, refusing to be known. You hide your pain, your confusion, your frustration, anger, and self-hatred—all the things that got you where you are and keep you there.

On the flip side, those who obsess about weight and food but do not *appear* overweight feel just as compelled to suffer alone because no one would know—to look at them—how much they wrestle in their minds and secret behaviors. They believe, often rightly, that people wouldn't understand their struggle. A person who appears to be a healthy weight can be in bondage as much as an obese person, but there is an opposite sort of discrimination that occurs when they try to join support groups or weight management programs. They're often asked derisively, "Why are you here?" and even demeaned and made to feel unwelcome. For the person who struggles with unhealthy food habits without being obviously overweight, the motivation to suffer alone and in secret is compelling.

## THINK ABOUT IT

The powerful principle driving the success of the numerous weight loss books and programs available is the magic bullet. We are all looking for that *one thing* that's going to finally work, the miracle cure that will unlock the mystery of our eating problems and allow us to solve them once and for all. Maybe cutting carbs is the answer. Maybe what we need is an exercise machine. Maybe we can pray our fat and cravings away.

But you know there's no magic involved, and you know it's not *one thing* that is going to change your life. It is going to be several different things put together. You are going to need to work on your life from every angle, and perhaps this is why weight and eating issues are so challenging. It's not about a diet or an exercise plan although these are crucial aspects. As the book *Lose It For Life* puts it, healing comes about through "a lifestyle of permanent weight management that emphasizes *the whole you: your spirit, mind, body, and emotions* (emphasis added)."[1]

Lose It For Life is a program (founded by New Life's Stephen Arterburn) that teaches this whole-person approach to weight loss and health. At Lose It For Life conferences, I've had the opportunity to speak to hundreds of despairing people who have had it up to *here* with their weight problems, and they are desperate for something new, something that works. One of the things I talk with them about is the idea that we are all hungry—but not necessarily for food. I joke that the conference is not *Lose* It For Life but *Starving* for Life. Sure, when you're dieting, you sometimes feel as though you're starving. But inside, many of us are simply starving for *life*, starving for meaning and purpose and relationships and good feelings. We are hungry, and we don't know how to satisfy our emptiness, so we stuff ourselves with food.

Most people are smart enough to know that's what they're doing even when they're doing it. But many have been emotionally eating for so long, it has become an automatic response, and they don't even know what their feelings are. It's like daydreaming while driving—you've arrived at your destination but can't remember anything about getting there. Therefore, simply being aware of your behavior isn't enough to change it. It's a place to start, but this isn't just a cognitive issue. Emotional eating has to do with your emotions, your past, your physical makeup, your mental attitude, and your spiritual life. It takes a multifaceted line of attack, which I like to call the Outside-In and Inside-Out approach.

On the Outside-In level, we deal with our symptoms: excess weight or extreme weight loss, inability to control our eating, the necessity of exercise or need to regulate compulsive exercise, and health issues related to obesity, binge-purge cycles, or restrictive eating and malnutrition.

On the Inside-Out level, we deal with the root issues, the things that are causing the symptoms. Obsession with weight and eating is always a symptom of other things going on in our lives. It's like having what you think is the common cold, but you can't get rid of it. You take decongestants and cough suppressants and sleeping aids to mask the symptoms so you can function, yet your cold never seems to go away. When you finally go to the doctor, you find out you have a nasty bacterial sinus infection. Your colds are not going to stop until you eradicate the germ that's causing all those unpleasant symptoms. You can look at your weight issues the same way. They're the symptoms. We need to find the germs that led to the development of those symptoms.

I'm betting that you know quite a lot about the Outside-In

approach. You know that a healthy diet is important along with the proper amount of exercise and health care to manage any other physical problems. It's the Inside-Out part that gets hard.

Inside-Out is about uncovering the secrets inside you—your pain, anxieties, insecurities, your past, your beliefs about yourself. The secrets have to come out if you are to heal—even the secrets you've been trying to keep from yourself. You see, in a strange way your weight and eating issues are *all about your secrets* and your attempts to avoid them.

One thing that has been proven time and time again is that it is virtually impossible to get out from under the tyranny of weight and food issues alone. You simply can't keep your secrets to yourself if you want to get better. Taking your problem out of the dark and bringing it to light by sharing it with God and others is crucial if you are going to change your life.

The good news is that there is no shortage of help available. And a variety of resources is what is needed. In my practice I help people who are stuck in food issues develop their own treatment team of support that includes doctors, nutritionists, support groups and therapy. There are accountability and support groups like Overeaters Anonymous and Weight Watchers. There are weight loss programs that involve one-on-one counseling as part of the plan. Many churches even have weight loss support groups or Celebrate Recovery eating issues groups. Joining with others for accountability and support can be very helpful if you *do the work required*. That means you don't just show up, but you engage, you share, you release your secrets in a safe environment while simultaneously working on the other areas in your life that need attention. The point of these groups is to get out of the habit of keeping everything to yourself.

Some people find that the safest place to begin coming out of isolation is through an online forum, message board, or chat room specifically for weight issues. If you spend time on the computer and you're not sure if you're ready to join a real-live group, check out some of the Internet resources listed at the end of this chapter. New Life has several Lose It For Life message boards where people share stories and encourage each other. This can be a wonderful introduction to the idea of uncovering your secrets as the first step to healing.

One of the best ways to begin addressing your root issues from the Inside-Out is to be in therapy with a therapist or psychologist who understands and works with eating disorders. Yes, it requires a commitment of resources, including time and money—but if you've been wrestling with your weight for years, then the commitment of resources might be not only worth it but also the only way you are going to find healing.

In therapy you can start looking at your childhood issues, whether they might involve abuse, abandonment, or emotional traumas. With the help of a caring professional, you can explore your self-concept, your anxieties, and the fears that keep you trapped in your food obsessions. You can ask yourself where your deprivation started and why you are so starving for life that you use food to fill yourself up and numb your pain.

When we are working hard on the Outside-In and the Inside-Out approaches, we can finally start to see things differently and begin to behave differently. It's only this hard work that leads to a paradigm shift, the *aha* moments where you get a new perspective on what's going on in your life. Here is where you find the motivation to change, day by day, hour by hour.

## SPIRITUAL SECRETS

This is what most of the weight-loss programs don't tell you: above all, you are dealing with a spiritual issue. Yes, it's also emotional, physical, psychological, and mental. But encompassing all of those is the overarching truth that you are a spiritual being, and your relationship with God and how you perceive His involvement in your life affects every single thing you think, feel, and do.

Programs such as Alcoholics Anonymous and Overeaters Anonymous, even though they are secular, have discovered the most important thing about recovering from any kind of addiction: admitting that you can't handle this on your own and that you must surrender to a "higher power." We know that we surrender not just to any random power but to the one true God, creator of heaven and earth, who is able to "accomplish infinitely more than we would ever dare to ask or hope" (Eph. 3:20 NLT). As Claire Cloninger says in her book *Faithfully Fit*, "Personally, I have found that anytime the buck stops with me and everything hinges on my inner resolve and fortitude, I am in big trouble!"[2]

Isn't that the truth? By now you must have realized that in your own strength and doing it your way, nothing is being accomplished. At least nothing *permanent*. Surrendering this problem to God means confessing that you have a problem, that your ways of handling it are not working, and that you are finished keeping this little secret all to yourself and are willing to move forward with Him toward healing. This is about "healing and wholeness and restoration—*healing* our self-images and our attitudes toward food, becoming *whole* people in Jesus Christ, and being *restored* to his design as children made in his image."[3]

Keeping our secret is a way of denying we have a problem. We hide from ourselves, God, and others the fact that we are hurting inside and that we have some real and profound fears and anxieties that need to be addressed. God can't work in us until we stop the denial, stop pretending, and surrender.

This is a spiritual battle taking place in your soul. Your number one task is to make sure God wins this battle—not the enemy and not you. You don't want your past to win or your anxieties or your pain. The goal is to let God win.

So how are you going to do this? Concentrating on a deeper relationship with God is the way to your new life. I particularly like the books *Lose It For Life* and *Faithfully Fit* since they approach weight management with the focus on your spiritual life, starting with surrender. Attending a Lose It For Life conference or intensive weekend can be an amazingly spiritual awakening as you begin to connect with God and others, starting to ease your pain through relationships rather than food. Being in a church-based weight-loss program and/or a Bible study where you can receive ongoing support and encouragement is valuable. Part of this journey of becoming free from weight and eating obsession is doing all the things you can to connect with yourself and God (as discussed in chapter 12).

## From Secrets to Solutions

This topic of obsessing over weight and food is so significant that I find it difficult to talk about it in such a brief format. The point here is not to give you all the answers but to remind you that this problem *cannot* be solved as long as it remains a secret from yourself, from God, or from others.

*Be honest with yourself.* You already know that you have some issues with food and eating. But now is the time to go deeper. Begin to explore what's underneath the surface of your obsession. Begin to identify the feelings you are trying to stuff down with food. Is there a secret you're keeping from yourself? Are you trying to avoid dealing with pain, anxiety, frustration, or insecurities? In the quiet of your own mind, perhaps while journaling, be as honest as you can about the secrets behind your secret.

*Be honest with God.* Pray about your obsession with food and weight. Confess your powerlessness over it. Explain your fears about tackling this problem in your life (the ones you're aware of at this point) and your sense of helplessness and hopelessness. Ask God to show you the meaning of surrender, to help you understand what this looks like in your life. Tell Him you want to surrender this problem completely to Him, but you will need His guidance. Commit to follow Him.

*Be honest with a friend, counselor, or support group.* The key to your recovery is this honesty with others (after first getting real with yourself and God) because it's in the context of real relationships that you will find hope and encouragement. God has created us for community, and it is through true connections with other believers that you will begin to truly understand and experience His profound love and care for you.

God wants you to find healing and wholeness. He wants you to experience true freedom. I encourage you to embark on this journey, trusting God and others to help you. Allow God to work in and through you, not depending on your strength but on His. I don't promise you this will be an easy path, but I promise you that you can find healing, once and for all.

## Praying Scripture for Your Secret

Pray Jeremiah 29:11 and 32:27.

> Lord, You have said that You know the plans You have for me, plans to prosper me and not to harm me, plans to give me hope and a future. Thank You for Your promise, Lord. I desperately need hope and a future. I ask You to show me where to find hope, and lead me into a brighter future. I pray for the faith to believe that You will work this in me, for You are the Lord, the God of all mankind. Nothing is too hard for You. It may be too hard for me alone, but not for You. I ask You now to work in me, and bring me to the future You desire for me. Amen.

## Recommended Resources

Internet
New Life—www.newlife.com
    Click on the Lose It For Life tab
National Eating Disorder Association—
    www.nationaleatingdisorders.org
To find an online community of support, Google
    "weight loss support groups"

## Support Groups

Celebrate Recovery—www.celebraterecovery.com
Overeaters Anonymous—www.oa.org
Weight Watchers—www.weightwatchers.com
National Association of Anorexia Nervosa and Associated
 Disorders—www.anad.org
  Eating disorder information and binge-eating included
Anorexia Nervosa and Related Eating Disorders, Inc.—
 www.anred.com
  Eating disorder information and binge-eating included
Remuda Ranch—www.remudaranch.com
  Christian eating disorder treatment programs for women and
  girls

## Books

*10 Essentials of Highly Healthy People* by Walt Larimore
*Faith and Fitness: Diet and Exercise for a Better World* by Tom P.
 Hafer
*Faithfully Fit: A 40-Day Devotional Plan to End the Yo-Yo Lifestyle of
 Chronic Dieting* by Claire Cloninger and Laura Barr
*Fat-Proof Your Family: God's Way to Forming Healthy Habits for Life*
 by J. Ron Eaker
*Layers* by Sandi Patty
*Lose It For Life: The Total Solution for Permanent Weight Loss* by
 Stephen Arterburn and Linda Mintle
*Love to Eat, Hate to Eat: Breaking the Bondage of Destructive Eating
 Habits* by Elyse Fitzpatrick
*Making Peace with Your Thighs: Get Off the Scales and Get On with
 Your Life* by Linda Mintle
*The Dieter's Prayer Book: Spiritual Power and Daily Encouragement*
 by Heather Kopp
*The Real Me* by Natalie Grant

# Chapter 16

# My Past Haunts Me

With counseling, I have come a long, long way in healing from childhood sexual abuse and being raped as an adult. However, I am still afraid that I will not be able to be sexually intimate with my husband (we marry in six months) unless it is totally dark. I realize that this is a "leftover" from all of my childhood trauma. I am a passionate woman, yet afraid that I will not be able to enjoy our physical intimacy.

◆ ◆ ◆

My deep secret is that I had two abortions in the '80s. The first was from ignorance; the second was from fear. It ended up bringing me to salvation in Jesus. I have lived these many years not telling more than three people.

◆ ◆ ◆

> I feel I need to share my secret, and it takes a lot of courage to do this. I'm married and have three children. My secrets are that prior to marriage, I was sexually intimate with maybe fifty men, and I had one abortion. It's so hard to say this!

If you've read the earlier chapters in this book, you've seen some of the terrible secrets many women struggle with. The unfortunate truth is that many of those secrets have their roots in the traumas of our past, the topic of this chapter. Everything from affairs and sexual addictions, to spiritual disconnection, to depression and eating disorders can stem from mistakes, sins, and suffering from long ago. These are the toughest issues, the ones that tend to make themselves known by masquerading as other problems. They are some of the hardest secrets to live with, and also some of the hardest to bring to light; but at the same time, living a full life requires them to come out of the darkness.

## UNLOCKING THE SECRET

The responses to our Secrets Blog revealed three major categories of past traumas that women carry around as hidden burdens. The first was sexual abuse in childhood—a tragedy that is so shockingly widespread it led psychologist Dr. Dan Allender to begin his book on recovering from sexual abuse, "At times, I wonder if every person in the world, male and female, young and old, has been sexually abused."[1] Sexual abuse in childhood has the potential to completely devastate a person's life. If kept bottled up and never dealt with, the consequences can seep into every aspect of living—relationships, jobs, emotional stability, and everyday functioning.

Another secret women carry about their past is the fact that they've had an abortion or, commonly, two. Considering there have been more than forty-five million abortions in the U.S. since 1973, it's not surprising that the Christian women responding to our survey reported this secret.[2] Most had their abortions when they were in their late teens or early twenties; some were Christians already, and others weren't. Regardless of when and why it occurred, the lasting effects of the abortion can plague women throughout their lives, especially if they never do any internal work of processing it.

The third major secret about the past is a woman's sexual history. Christian women are carrying tremendous guilt for the decisions they made long ago although their experiences vary tremendously. Some are feeling guilty for the decision to have sex with their husband prior to marriage (this was mostly reported by women whose only lifetime sex partner has been the husband to whom each is still married). Others reported sexual promiscuity and the consequences that can come with it, including disease, unplanned pregnancies, and emotional devastation.

The past is weighing heavily on us. Why aren't more women doing something about it?

## Keeping the Secret

The good part about the traumas of our past is that those events are in the past. The worst is over and done with. But the bad part is that they're never really gone. And for some women, their whole lives become internally organized around these events. You can spend years of your life and tons of emotional energy pretending your past doesn't exist, but that doesn't make it go away. Ironically, the only thing that lessens the past's negative effect on your present is to look directly at it—examining it, processing it, feeling the old feelings again, grieving the losses of innocence, and choosing to change your response to it. But if that's true, then why do so many people choose not to face their demons?

For most people, it's just too scary. Looking back at your own mistakes and sins, or the heinous sins committed against you, has the potential to completely upend your life and often the lives of those around you. If you are accustomed to quietly stuffing your pain, acting as if everything is okay, and living a fairly productive life, you have every reason to want to avoid a disruption. Instinctively you know that to face your past would mean reliving it somehow, dredging up the guilt and shame and fear and confusion and anger. You are afraid your very life will unravel if you face this part of your past, and you may well be right. You keep your secret to preserve and protect yourself and your loved ones from the possible calamitous consequences of bringing it into the open.

Your shame is a major factor that keeps you from wanting anyone else to know your secret. You've come a long way since then—a long way since you were the hideously abused child, or a long way since you made the sinful choices—and part of you can't reconcile that old you with who you are today. It just doesn't fit anymore, so sometimes you even convince yourself that it wasn't really *you* back then. It was somehow a different person, someone else's life story. You may have even mastered the art of being so detached from it that you can talk about it as if relaying data about someone you only remotely know. You carry the secret because you have almost convinced yourself it didn't really happen.

## THINK ABOUT IT

If you are carrying one of these past traumas, my heart goes out to you. I have done intense psychotherapy with many women in your situation, and I'm aware of the pain you might be experiencing. But I've seen women take the risk and do the work of digging up their secrets from the past, and I've seen them come out the other side with a new and joyful approach to life.

Rebecca was a woman in her forties who had survived years of incest as a child, and as an adult she had a conflicted but ongoing relationship with the father who had abused her. As a result, she struggled with compulsive overeating, was overweight, and while she appeared "together" in her professional life, had lifelong relational difficulties. She got the courage to go into counseling and began the hard work of processing her feelings and seeing the truth about what had happened to her, and eventually she was able to join a survivors' support group and attend a weeklong intensive workshop for adult survivors of childhood sexual abuse. All of these were situations in which Rebecca was able to talk about her abuse, vent about it, express her feelings honestly, and assess the damage it had done to her life. Rebecca finally felt the chains breaking and began to extricate herself from the bondage of her past. Over the next several months, she moved far away from her father and told him he was on his own, and she began to break free from her eating disorder as well. Years later, Rebecca has a solid marriage and a good life, and she no longer defines herself according to the abuse she endured as a child. She now helps other women heal from the same type of history.

But not all stories have a happy ending. Judy is in her early sixties and suffered similar sexual abuse as a child. She, too, developed an eating disorder as a way to cope (very common with sexual trauma) and avoided all kinds of close relationships. She has gone through her adult life stuffing the pain of her childhood, never telling anyone about the abuse. Her mother has had a chronic debilitating illness for as long as Judy can remember. Thus, her mother was self-focused and too much in need of her own care to care for Judy. As an only child, Judy felt burdened by the demand of her aging and ailing parents. By the time her abusive father died, ten years ago, she'd never confronted him and still never told anyone what he'd done. If she were to tell her mother now, who is frail and in the later stages of dementia, she fears the truth would literally kill her or she wouldn't remember an hour later, and that would emotionally crush Judy. These secrets have infiltrated her entire life, her work, and every relationship she's ever had. The abuse defined her and made her feel insecure and inadequate so that she never had the confidence to create a real life for herself. At nearly retirement, she has never had a husband or children and has kept friends at arm's length; her two cats are her faithful companions. She doesn't feel connected to others and has a sense of unfulfillment. Now for the first time, she is in therapy to deal with this lifetime of tragedy and pain, but she is infused with a sense of hopelessness. She feels it may be too late to really "get a life." Only now, when she's finally started opening up about the pain of her past, does she realize that the keeping of this secret has literally shattered her life.

It's heartbreaking, yes. But I want you to hear these stories to get across the crucial point: as painful as it is . . . as unthinkable as it might be . . . you have to talk to someone about the pain in your past to avoid letting it destroy your chance for happiness and a fulfilling life.

Your past doesn't have to define you, whether it was filled with unspeakable acts committed against you, or poor and immoral choices made by you. But it will define you if you don't deal with those issues.

Sometimes people do a really good job of acting as if their past traumas never happened, and they create productive, highly functioning lives for themselves. But there is usually a point of reckoning, a time at which the old ways of coping don't work anymore. It's as if you're a container, and emotionally you are just stuffing things in your whole life. Eventually the container is full and starts running over. The things you used to stuff are going to start leaking out into your life. You can only stuff for so long before you have to deal with your pain.

It's possible, however, to be overly focused on the past. While some people try to ignore it or pretend it never existed, others wallow in it, blame everything in their lives on the past, and define themselves by it. This is just as unhealthy as ignoring it. The point of dealing with your past is to process it in a healthy way and eventually be able to break free of it. Will there always be scars? Probably. But a scar that has nicely healed over is vastly preferable to a festering, infected wound.

## SPIRITUAL SECRETS

Whatever past trauma you are carrying around, you may feel a profound sense of shame. You might also be feeling guilt, fear, humiliation, dishonor, and a pervading experience of being unclean or contaminated. Whether your past shame involves sexual abuse, sexual promiscuity, abortion, or anything else, you feel tainted by it.

This is not what God wants for you. He isn't honored or glorified when we stay in our shame and remain in bondage to the sin (whether we committed it, or it was perpetrated on us). God wants us to experience His healing. First John 1:9 says, "If we confess our sins, he is faithful and just and will forgive us our sins and *purify us from all unrighteousness*" (emphasis added). This means we can be cleansed from whatever wrongs we did, as well as any wrongs that were committed against us. God promises to purify us.

Is guilt a part of your picture? Women who acted out sexually or had abortions usually carry a pretty significant boatload of guilt. Even people who were abused as children carry some type of guilt because they "let it happen" or because they experienced normal physical responses as a result of the molestation. Confess it to God and accept His gift of cleansing.

The enemy loves nothing more than for us to stay in bondage to our guilt and shame, neglecting to accept the healing and love of our Lord. This is one way he keeps us from glorifying God, showing Jesus to others, and living joyful lives of freedom. You cannot change your past, but you can choose to reject the enemy's ploys. You can choose to change your response to your situation, refuse to be driven by the past, and take steps to begin the long, hard process of forgiveness.

Perhaps the most important key to your healing process will be forgiveness. Without it, you won't have peace. It doesn't take away the hurts of the past; neither does it condone actions, but it takes away their power to control and destroy your life. Who do you need to forgive? Is it your abuser? Is it yourself? There may be several other people in your life who somehow allowed or enabled your trauma to take place—the mother who turned a blind eye to your plight, the boyfriend who insisted on the abortion. It may even be God for not stepping in as you thought He should or could. Think of each person you still harbor blame toward. These are the people you'll need to work on forgiving as you go down this road of unpacking and leaving behind your past.

Forgiveness is a process; it's not a one-time decision. That's why it's so hard to deal with it. In order to truly forgive, you have to go back into the pain, and it's going to get messy and painful—but you can survive it. The only way to the other side of this minefield of past traumas is *through* it. You can't go around it.

In his book, *Forgiving the Unforgivable*, David Stoop wrote:

> Forgiveness always involves the moral side of life. It involves our sense of right and wrong, of fairness, and of justice. It also involves our sense of love, compassion and mercy. When someone violates us with a seemingly unforgivable act, at least some of these values have been violated.
>
> We then experience an internal conflict over how to resolve the conflict. For example, when someone we love betrays us, our values of right and wrong—or fairness—and of justice cry out for satisfaction. But we are torn, for there is another part of us that holds on to feelings of love for that person, compassion for their predicament, and a desire to show mercy. We are angry because of the tension between these two sets of values, which are competing for our attention. If we are to forgive, it feels like we must deny our own sense of justice and fairness. But *not* to forgive is to deny our sense of love and compassion. There is no easy way out of the predicament.[3]

This holds true even if the person you are trying to forgive is yourself. C. S. Lewis wrote, "I think that if God forgives us we must forgive ourselves. Otherwise it is almost like setting ourselves up as a higher tribunal than Him."[4] It's not going to be easy. But in the end, forgiveness of your abuser, any enablers, and yourself is vital before you can find peace.

It's obvious the path ahead of you—the journey of letting your secrets out, processing your pain, and forgiving—will be difficult to excruciating at times. You may even think at this point that there is no way you could ever forgive. So why bother? Why not just stay in your comfortable world of denial and avoidance? Well, first, because your world isn't really all that comfortable, is it? You are missing out on the fullness of life. And in the words of Dan Allender, "The answer is simple: to live out the gospel. The reason for entering the struggle is a *desire for more, a taste of what life and love could be if freed from the dark memories and deep shame* (emphasis added)."[5]

Doesn't that sound as though it would be worth it?

## From Secrets to Solutions

The actual process of working through past traumas that haunt you is much more complicated than I could ever convey in one chapter of a book, so that hasn't been my goal. My purpose here has been to let you know you're not alone if your life has been devastated, to whatever small or large extent, by things you did in the past or things that have been done to you. And I want you to know that healing will come when you take a stand against all that and refuse to keep it locked inside any longer.

*Be honest with yourself.* Do you recognize anything familiar in these pages? If so, admit it in your own mind and heart, right now. Grab a journal or a piece of paper and begin to jot down some of your initial thoughts and feelings. Don't censor, and don't talk yourself out of them. What brings you shame? What makes you feel dirty, bad, unworthy? How has it affected your life? How do you feel right now? Write down what you're afraid of. If you were to tell someone about this, what do you fear will happen?

*Be honest with God.* Pray about this issue in your life, using the notes you just wrote. Confess any part of it that was sin. Ask to be purified and washed clean right this very moment. Tell God your fears, hurts, and anger, and then tell Him you want to be free. Ask Him to lead you to freedom, and thank Him that you can or are willing to take a step of faith to trust Him to do so.

*Be honest with a psychologist, therapist, or Christian support group.* This may be your hardest step, but as you know by now, it's a vital one. There is no book that can walk you through this process, and you probably won't be able to handle it "between you and God." You need the support, encouragement, and wisdom of other humans. You need to shed your secrets in an environment of love and acceptance, and learn who you really are as reflected back to you by others. I have seen many people find healing and freedom this way. Please use the list below, as well as any local church or ministry resources in your area, and find someone with whom you can talk.

## Praying Scripture for Your Secret

Pray Isaiah 43:18–19.

> Lord, help me to do as You say, *forget the former things.* Help me not to dwell on the past. Show me that You are doing a new thing! Let me watch as it springs up in my life; if I do not perceive it, please show me. You have promised to make a way in my desert and provide refreshing streams in my wasteland. I am ready, Lord! I am ready for Your healing. Please bring me to a place of peace and comfort, and let me experience Your joy. Amen.

## Recommended Resources

### Internet
New Life—www.newlife.com
    Click on the Healing-Is-a-Choice tab
Adult Survivors of Child Abuse——www.ascasupport.org
Rachel's Vineyard Ministries—www.rachelsvineyard.org
    Post-abortion healing with retreats in many states
After Abortion Counseling—Pregnancy Care Centers—
    http://pregnancycenters.org
    1-800-395-HELP

Abortion Recovery Network—www.abortionrecoverynetwork.org

## Books

*Can't Keep Silent: A Woman's 22-Year Journey of Post-Abortion Healing* by Lydia A. Clark

*Choosing Forgiveness: Your Journey to Freedom* by Nancy Leigh DeMoss

*Forgive and Forget: Healing the Hurts We Don't Deserve* by Lewis B. Smedes

*Forgiven and Set Free: A Post-Abortion Bible Study for Women* by Linda Cochrane

*Forgiveness Is a Choice: A Step-by-Step Process for Resolving Anger and Restoring Hope* by Robert D. Enright

*Forgiving Our Parents, Forgiving Ourselves* by Dave Stoop and James Masteller

*Forgiving the Unforgivable* by Dave Stoop

*Healing for Damaged Emotions Workbook* by Beth Funk

*Her Choice to Heal: Finding Spiritual and Emotional Peace After Abortion* by Sydna Masse with Joan Phillips

*On the Threshold of Hope* by Diane Mandt Langberg

*Redeeming the Past: Recovering from the Memories that Cause Our Pain* by David A. Seamands

*Shattered Dreams: God's Unexpected Pathway to Joy* by Larry Crabb

*The Healing Path: How the Hurts in Your Past Can Lead You to a More Abundant Life* by Dan B. Allender

*The Search for Significance: Seeing Your True Worth Through God's Eyes* by Robert McGee

*The Wounded Heart: Hope for Adult Victims of Childhood Sexual Abuse* by Dan B. Allender

*This Wasn't Supposed to Happen to Me* by Bev Smallwood

*You're Not Alone: Healing Through God's Grace After Abortion* by Jennifer O'Neill

*Part Six*

# SECRETS ABOUT PERSONAL ISSUES

Chapter 17

# I Worry About Finances

Since my husband is totally incapable of managing money, and since I am in charge of paying bills and all the finances, I have a secret savings account to help us in times of need. If he knew we had any money, he would spend it immediately. One time we were having problems and he threatened to leave, but then ordered me to leave. I thought I should have an emergency fund if anything like that should happen again. So maybe this savings account would just save me.

◆ ◆ ◆

I struggle with being a single parent. I am a widow and I am spending the life insurance money at a rapid speed, possibly jeopardizing my children's and my future. I don't seem to have control over it, and I don't know where to go. No one has been able to help me.

✦ ✦ ✦

I am afraid we will live in poverty forever and not be able
to break out. Even though along the way I have seen God
provide for us in wonderful ways. It hurts to always be two
months behind on the utility bill and always getting disconnect notices. It hurts that I cannot afford to send my
oldest son to school when he is so bright, but he has to
work two jobs in order to make his vehicle payments. I
want so much better for my kids than what I have had.

Every economic indicator in our country tells us that Americans
struggle with financial issues—lack of money, wanting more
money, rising debt, fear, and fatalism about money. Statistics show
us that consumer debt is at an all-time high. Churches have a hard
time getting people to tithe. *Most people* have some sort of financial
concern in their life. So I found it interesting that, compared to many
of our other secrets, only a few women wrote to the Secrets Blog
about their financial burdens.

As difficult as it is to believe, it may be that *money* is the ultimate
secret. It seems crazy, considering we've been talking about everything from adultery to sexual addiction to child abuse. But the issue
of finances just might be one of the last conversational taboos in
polite society.

---

## Unlocking the Secret

Financial expert Suze Orman wrote about her first taste of success working at a large financial institution. "I was rich, richer than
I could have imagined," she said, "and I realized I was profoundly
unhappy; the money hadn't bought or brought happiness."[1]

Christian financial guru Larry Burkett reported a similar discovery early in his career (before he was a Christian): "Even though I
was making more money than I'd ever made before, somehow it

didn't seem to make me any happier. Since I had come from a poor family, I had always believed that money would be the answer. It wasn't that I was going to spend the money; I was sure that just having it would make me feel better. But it didn't."[2]

And Jesus told us, "A man's life does not consist in the abundance of his possessions" (Luke 12:15).

Do you notice a theme developing here? The main reason we worry about money is because we believe—falsely—that it will bring us a greater level of happiness, peace, or contentment. But it turns out the old adage is true: money doesn't buy happiness.

The biggest reason for having financial problems is that we start out with misleading beliefs about money—what it can and can't do for us, what it says about us, and whether we have power over it or it has power over us. The financial concerns that women wrote to our Secrets Blog about, and those we hear from people on the radio at New Life as well as the people who come into my office, all come down to some basic issues:

+ Money is thought of as a big problem (and often becomes that), but usually it's a symptom of a deeper problem.

+ We expect money to provide us with things it can't: peace, freedom from fear, a better marriage, deeper joy in life.

+ People are often fatalistic and pessimistic about their financial problems, saying things like, "I've tried everything," when in fact they haven't, or "Nobody can help me," when there is actually help available.

+ Like every other area of life, people make unwise decisions about finances. Yet the answer doesn't lie in beating yourself up over it, but in getting help to solve the problem.

+ Fears about money and in particular, the future, block realistic thinking, planning, and wise decision making.

+ Our culture encourages greed, making financial strongholds a favorite tactic of the enemy.

In my many years working in psychiatric hospital programs, treatment settings, and clinical private practice, I have found that many bright, educated, and talented women have a profound fear of ending up homeless or in poverty. While this surprised me in my early intern years, I've found it to be a common persistent theme and have a greater appreciation now for the depth of their fear. In terms of our attitudes toward money, there are significant gender differences. We already know that men and women are different, as many hundreds of authors have written about, and that because our brains are hardwired differently, we approach life, relationships, and money differently.

Olivia Mellan, psychotherapist and money coach, wrote about these attitudes in her article "Money and Gender." She discussed the fact that women tend to grow up underconfident about money, believing that "they won't be good at the money stuff" and, hopefully, can marry a rich man or have someone else take care of it. Men, on the other hand, are usually treated, from boyhood on, as if they will be good with money whether they learn much about it or not. Many men, therefore, are overconfident when it comes to the handling or investing of money, and especially if they earn the majority of it, feel they should be in charge. After all, since men are generally more competitive and women more relational, they have won the money race.

Christian men often feel it is their God-given position to be in charge of finances, and most Christian women believe this, too, even if they are better money handlers than their partners. Mellan cited a Liberty Mutual study of junior high and high school students to measure their self-perception of knowledge of math and money. The boys said, "we know a lot" while the girls stated, "we don't know much"—while in actuality, they performed at the same level of expertise.[3]

Money is a much bigger issue than we generally give it credit for (pardon the pun!). It's a part of life every single day, and our feelings, thoughts, fears, and expectations about it come from deep inside us and go all the way back to childhood. It's something we all deal with, so why do people keep finances such a big secret?

## Keeping the Secret

Imagine being in church and your pastor announces that several members are going to give their testimonies in today's service. You sit back and prepare yourself for stories of wayward lives put back on track by Jesus, lost children found through prayer, addictions cured through faith in God . . . dramatic tales of rescue common in the testimonies of believers.

But when the people stand up to speak, this is what you hear:

"My wife and I ran up twenty thousand dollars' worth of credit card bills, and now we can't pay our bills. If we don't get some relief soon, I'm afraid we will lose our house."

"I'm a single mom trying to make ends meet. I have no money for my kids to go to college and no money for my own retirement. I fear what's going to happen in the future."

"My husband and I fight all the time about money. I don't know how we're going to make this marriage last. It's miserable."

"My wife doesn't know I stash money into a secret bank account. I don't even know why I do it. Just want some independence, I guess."

Well, you get the picture. The point is—nothing like this *ever* happens. We simply don't tell people our financial troubles. To be fair, we're not supposed to talk about *positive* money issues either, like how much we make, how much we spent on our house, or what we paid for the car. It's thought of as tacky or bragging if you do. Money talk is simply taboo.

Even when churches ask for prayer for their members, you'll see requests like this one: "John Smith lost his job due to layoffs. Please pray for the Smith family's provision and a new job for John." But you *never* see, "John Smith bought a bass boat and too many fishing supplies over the last few years, and now the family is up to their ears in debt. Please pray for God to provide a way out."

Doesn't the thought of it make you cringe?

Our society has a hard time being honest about financial issues, but it's even more complex for Christians because on the whole, we tend to have unrealistic (and unbiblical) attitudes about money. We think we're not supposed to pay attention to it, that "money is the root of all evil" (a misreading of Scripture), and that it's somehow bad to think about money, talk about it, manage it, and work to make more of it.[4] We spend incredible amounts of time and energy worrying about it while pretending we don't.

Another problem for Christians is that we tend to think that our financial problems are caused by sin—or at least, that *others* will think they are. We feel cautious about admitting our money concerns because we just know someone's going to ask us, "Are you sure you don't have any unconfessed sin in your life? Maybe that's why you are struggling." Whether you do or don't, it's not what you need to hear. One woman I know who has a knack for maximizing every inch of her house confessed to a friend that when she was mad at her husband, she would spend money to get back at him. Her friend responded by saying, "Gee, there must be a lot of anger and discontent in this house!"

The truth is some financial problems are caused by sin (such as greed or disobedience), and others have different causes, such as ignorance, medical problems, or unexpected circumstances. Financial issues are not a better indicator of sin than anything else, but still, we hold back because it feels as if it leaves us open to judgment by others.

Many Christians have fascinating testimonies about being saved by Jesus after all manner of tragedy, sin, and immoral living. Those same people may be drowning in debt or overwhelmed by anxiety about their financial future, but you'd never know it.

One of the saddest parts of this is that our culture's money secrecy has led countless people to hide their financial truth from their spouses, children, and even themselves. We bring our money-related behavior underground, operating in the dark, working hard to keep it a covert operation. But the secrecy itself is compounding the problem.

## THINK ABOUT IT

Debbie grew up in a family with parents who constantly conveyed they didn't have enough money. Her mom penny-pinched, clipped coupons, and bought the children thrift-store clothing except for the ones she sewed herself. Debbie wasn't able to take dance lessons or gymnastics with her friends because it was *too expensive*. Vacations were always at a local campground, and Debbie's family ate in restaurants only about once a year. Meanwhile, the family moved several times, each time to a bigger house in a more expensive neighborhood. Yet the attitude was still always the same, no matter what Debbie asked for: "We can't afford it." Talk about mixed messages! Debbie began feeling resentful that she was always being denied the normal things kids in her neighborhood had. She couldn't care less about the big houses.

Years later when Debbie was an adult, her parents divorced. Her father promptly retired and proceeded to spend the next dozen years (and counting) traveling the world. All Debbie can think about is those awful thrift-store clothes, and she wonders why she was set up for a lifetime of feeling poor when her family clearly wasn't. She can see now that her dad was stashing the money away, presumably for retirement, but clearly there was plenty of it, considering his present lifestyle. Debbie carried a few important lessons about money into adulthood with her, including these:

+ There is never enough for what I want.
+ You can never really know for sure what's going on in the money situation. It's very confusing.
+ People hide money and don't talk about it.
+ People use money to have power and keep control over others.

Regardless of the relative truth of any of these statements, they completely determine the way Debbie approaches money today.

And this is true for all of us. Our attitudes about money and how we relate to it go all the way back to childhood, where we received the messages that control our financial lives.

Many people's attitudes toward money are characterized by worry and fear, and this started in childhood as well. However, as with every secret we've talked about in this book, we will never solve our financial problems and have a healthy attitude about money until we bring those fears and anxieties out of the closet and hold them up to the light. Most people deal with money by avoiding it. They spend without regard to their incomes; they get into financial trouble but don't research the available resources to help them.

The key to getting on top of your finances is, first, being honest with yourself—a key component of every single chapter of this book. I had to laugh when I realized that step three of Suze Orman's *9 Steps to Financial Freedom* is "Being honest with yourself." Money is scary for most of us, so being honest and facing our real attitudes and behaviors can be difficult.

As with all the other secrets we've discussed, the surface problem—in this case financial issues—is usually a reflection of a deeper issue in our lives. Money troubles definitely become big problems in their own right, but the way they got that way tells you what kind of difficulty you had before the money became an issue. Perhaps the problem was simple ignorance of how to manage money; likely it was something deeper. The original problem could have been any number of things, from living above your means (difficulty saying no to yourself, entitlement, envy) to covering up other painful issues in your life (low self-esteem, anger, emptiness) through spending, to having control issues or a power struggle in your marriage (passive-aggressive revenge, need for separateness). Just as in the sexual arena, couples play out their marital dynamics in the financial arena as well, and children take their perceived socioeconomic status into their adult lives regardless of the balance of their bank accounts. You might find a way to solve your surface problem (by acquiring more money in the short term), but until you dig into the depths and discover the dynamics that caused the problem in the first place, you are going to keep creating it over and over again.

It's easy to gain insight about all of this and still avoid *doing* anything about it. Even if you put into motion a plan for financial restoration, it's easy to become discouraged when you realize there are no miracle cures, no quick fixes, and that this is going to take a while. How are you going to make the leap from hearing and understanding to doing? And once you do, how are you going to push past discouragement and continue the journey to financial freedom for as long as it takes?

1. Spend some time thinking about your childhood, and identify any money-related memories. Make a list of the thoughts and feelings that came from those. See if you can make the connection between what you learned in your formative years and how you handle money today.

2. Look honestly at your financial situation right now. Write down all your debts, all your ongoing bills, and your expected monthly income. Get a realistic picture of where you are. While some of you may be pleasantly surprised that your financial picture is not as bad as you thought, be aware that for many people, the initial response will likely be discouragement. It often doesn't seem plausible on paper, yet most of us aren't starving. Learning can only happen if you take off your avoidance glasses and look. Not looking is a sure plan for financial disaster. Remember knowledge (although it's not money) is power.

3. Make a plan for the future. This step could take weeks or months because I want you to avail yourself of every possible resource to learn what you need to know and get help out of your money pit. Check out books from the library. Join a financial management Bible study. Make an appointment with a certified financial planner, a debt reduction advisor, or whatever professional is appropriate for you. Check out Debtors Anonymous (DA)—it's free, with helpful insight and accountability.

Whatever you do, avoid getting trapped in the nobody-can-help-me;-I'm-beyond-hope cycle. There is help and hope for everyone.

The key is looking at your money straight on and realizing that it is within your power to decide how to manage it and use it. Face your fears from the past, and then look unflinchingly at your present reality and make a plan for moving forward.

However, I'm going to be totally honest with you. This isn't going to be enough. You also need to look at what the Bible says about money and how your management of it speaks volumes about your spiritual life, your priorities, and your relationship to God.

## SPIRITUAL SECRETS

> I don't feel secure with my husband's earnings from his nonprofit, Christian job. I hide money in the house and in a bank account to bail us out if we need money for an emergency. My dad always hid money as I was growing up, and I began to store money away too. I want to have more faith in God and my husband to provide for us. I'm hoping to increase my faith walk.

This woman was brave to spill her secret, and her letter illustrates an important principle. She learned to hide money in her family of origin; in fact, her whole perspective of needing to hide money in case of an emergency came from her dad's lack of trust. This is deeper than simply being financially cautious. I'm willing to bet that this woman has other issues in her life related to lack of trust and fears about the future.

The wonderful thing is that she has recognized that this is a faith issue and is sincerely trying to do something about it. She is approaching it on the deepest level—that of her faith in God. And this is where we all need to look, in order to unravel our complex attitudes about our financial lives.

Many Christians believe that God doesn't care very much about money and that we shouldn't focus on it. But there are more than seven hundred verses in the Bible directly and specifically referring to money.[5] What do all these verses tell us about money? The bottom line is *wisdom*. We should be wise in handling our money.

+ We are to save money, but not hoard it.

+ We are to spend money, but with discretion and control.

+ We are to give back to the Lord, joyfully and sacrificially.

+ We are to use our money to help others, but with discernment and the guidance of God's Spirit.

+ It is not wrong to be rich, but it is wrong to love money.

+ It is not wrong to be poor, but it is wrong to waste money on trivial things.[6]

One of the worst problems plaguing Americans today is consumer debt. I believe the enemy is using our greed and our culture's consumer orientation to destroy families and to keep Christians defeated and down in the dumps. The only way to stand against this destruction is to go back to the Bible, learn its principles, and do our best to follow them.

It's really not so much about our money—how much of it we have and how much we need. It's more about whether we are taking the right approach. Jesus said not to worry about tomorrow, but to instead seek first His kingdom and His righteousness (Matt. 6:31–33). First work on your spiritual life, learning to trust God and seek Him in all things. Peace of mind comes from God, not from a healthy bank account.

If you're plagued with worry, your first task is to surrender that worry over to God as often as necessary. As Larry Burkett wrote, "Number one, confess that it's not your responsibility, turn it over to Jesus, and trust Him. Trust is the only cure for worry. *'Casting all your anxiety upon him, because he cares for you'* (1 Peter 5:7). Do what you can to prepare for the future and let God do the rest."[7]

If you're really demoralized by finances, you might perceive these as nothing more than spiritual platitudes. You may ask how reading Scripture and turning to God can give you more money now. But the Bible is clear on these issues. God requires we put our trust in Him, and He promises to provide for us if we let Him. God's timing as well as His definition of a crisis is different from ours. He knows what we need and may use our financial crisis to grow us if we are willing. Ask Him to shift your focus to what He has for you instead of what you believe you need.

I can't end this discussion without talking about the idea of our tithe, or our giving to the church and to charity. When people are in financial difficulty, perceived or real, often the first thing to go is the tithe. You've probably heard the sermon in church as many times as I have, so I'm not going to give you one. Let me just remind you that your tithe is an offering from your heart, an expression of where you are spiritually, and a tangible symbol of your total trust in God for the outcome (and income) of your life. In other words, this is a heart issue, not a legalism issue. As you are assessing your financial situation, make your giving a priority. Ask God to lead you in this, and you can trust that He will provide the wisdom.

Above all, remember that everything we have is a gift from God. We are merely caretakers of it all—money and everything else in creation. Deal with your money issues first by expressing thanks that God has allowed you to take part in caring for all He has made.

Finally, let's keep things in perspective. Money is not the most important thing in life. I'm not denying that the lack of it can make things miserable. But true joy is found through relationship, both with God and with family and friends. Make God and people your priority, and be wise about your handling of money. God will honor that, and He will be faithful to provide for you.

## From Secrets to Solutions

If you are holding secrets about financial issues, I want to warn you that the road to freedom will not be simple. The way out from a money crisis is usually not quick; it takes work and discipline. However, God doesn't intend for you to do this alone. He will be there for you, and if you need earthly assistance, He will be faithful to provide that too.

*Be honest with yourself.* This is where you need to do the things I suggested above. Look at your childhood and your history with money, and try to understand how you got where you are today. Take responsibility for your attitudes and actions first in your own heart without excuses. Look at how you handle your money, and listen to what it's telling you about your values and priorities. Write down your fears. Assess your current situation. Only when you get real with what's really going on will you be able to move forward with clear direction.

*Be honest with God.* Confess any sin that has led you here. Explain your fears about the future. Ask God to increase your faith and trust in Him, and ask Him for wisdom on how to proceed. Ask also that He would send someone or something to help you and guide you. Commit to following His direction.

*Be honest with someone else.* If you are hiding debt or stashing money without your spouse's knowledge, it may be time to come clean with this. Depending on your husband's personality, consider doing it in the presence of a marriage counselor. The secrecy indicates you have some marital issues to work out anyway, so a therapist is a good place to start. If you can't start with your spouse, or if you are single and not ready to confide in a friend, then consider an anonymous support group, such as Debtors Anonymous, to build your courage.

Consider also professional financial counseling. It's difficult when your finances are already a mess, but sometimes you have to spend just a little bit more to get yourself on the right road.

There are numerous other helps available, from online financial ministries, to Bible studies on finances, even radio programs that can help increase your awareness of money-related issues. I encourage you to face it head-on, approaching it on as many fronts as necessary, to find freedom from this burdensome secret.

## Praying Scripture for Your Secret

Pray Matthew 6:31–33.

> Father, You have told us not to worry, so I ask You to help me avoid saying, "What shall we eat?" or "What shall we drink?" or "What shall we wear?" For people who do not know You run after all these things, but You, heavenly Father know that we need them. Please teach me and remind me to seek first Your kingdom and Your righteousness, and help me to trust and believe that when I do, all necessary things will be given to me as well. Amen.

## Recommended Resources

### Internet
Crown Financial Ministries—www.crown.org
> Click on "Radio" to find the radio programs in your area or listen online

### Support Groups
Debtors Anonymous—www.debtorsanonymous.org
> Check Web site for twelve-step support groups in your area or online meetings

Clutters Anonymous—www.clutterersanonymous.net
> Twelve-step support and literature for hoarding/spending issues and help with clearing out emotional clutter

Check with your local church for Christian based support groups or financial stewardship classes

### Books
*A Mom's Guide to Family Finances* by Ellie Kay
*Biblical Financial Study* by Crown Financial Ministries Staff
*Debt-Proof Your Marriage: How to Achieve Financial Harmony* by Mary Hunt

*Mastering Money in Your Marriage* by Ron Blue

*Miserly Moms: Living on One Income in a Two-Income Economy* by Jonni McCoy

*Money Matters* by Larry Burkett

*Money Shy to Money Sure: A Woman's Road Map to Financial Well-Being* by Olivia Mellan and Sherry Christie

*Money Talks and So Can We* by Ron Blue, Judy Blue, Jodie Berndt

*Profit Sharing: The Chapman Guide to Making Money an Asset in Your Marriage* by Gary Chapman

*The 9 Steps to Financial Freedom* by Suze Orman

*The Total Money Makeover* by Dave Ramsey

*Women and Money: Owning the Power to Control Your Destiny* by Suze Orman

# Chapter 18

# I Struggle with Alcohol or Drug Addiction

The problem is I drink just about every night, and nobody knows it. It consumes my every thought. Knowing what I need to do and not doing it. Hiding it, lying, my relationship with God, it is all so overwhelming. The shame of getting caught.

◆ ◆ ◆

I believe I might be an alcoholic. It started with a glass of wine in the evening to help me unwind. Now I can drink up to two bottles without being able to relax.

I am a born-again Christian and a church leader. I am on the worship team and regularly lead worship. I am the director of the church food bank. I work full time and still manage to drink and maintain my responsibilities. But I am slipping, and I know it. I feel sick all the time, but no one knows. I don't know where to turn. There is no one to confess this to, no one who is safe.

I've heard people, including the pastor, speaking critically of people with addiction problems, which is why I've been unable to confess this to anyone. When they find out, I will be labeled. I know others who have been honest about their problems. I have watched those people slowly be rejected, disrespected, and ultimately isolated by leadership and the body, in spite of their efforts to get clean. If they knew about me, it would be even be worse because I am in leadership.

I wish I could go to a recovery center, but if I left for any period of time, it would be impossible to keep it a secret. I have prayed and prayed about this but have not seen any breakthrough.

◆ ◆ ◆

Right now I'm on Vicodin and alcohol. It's not good, but I do it to escape most Saturdays when I'm alone. It's my fault because I isolate, so I don't blame anyone. I choose it, but I'm not proud of it.

Did you ever see the movie *When a Man Loves a Woman* with Andy Garcia and Meg Ryan? It portrays a middle-class family—the father is an airline pilot, the mother a middle school counselor—that looks perfectly normal from the outside. But Alice, the mother (Meg Ryan), is an alcoholic who drinks all day, every day. She has managed to put on an effective facade for a long time, but as her drinking increases, she begins to slip. One day she goes out drinking with a friend after school and forgets to come home to her family until after midnight. Another time, obviously drunk, she slaps her daughter and then passes out on the bathroom floor amid crashing glass and blood. It takes some extreme episodes like this for both her and her husband to realize that she desperately needs help.

Alcoholism and drug addiction often play out like this in families across the country. Women manage to hide it effectively—up to a point. But eventually things spiral out of control, and something's got to give. That's when the full extent of the secret comes out.

## Unlocking the Secret

It starts with an innocent second glass of wine with dinner, which becomes a third, and repeats night after night. It continues as you find you are desperate for the relief that alcohol brings, and one day you're looking at the clock, anxiously awaiting 5 p.m. There comes another day when it's only three o'clock, but you hear yourself say, "It's five o'clock somewhere" as you break out the alcohol. Or you tell yourself that it's not a problem because, after all, you're not drinking every day, just on special occasions or on especially tough days or when you're feeling down and just need to get through. You can go days without a drink and not even think about it, but then life gets a little stressful again, and the alcohol helps. You know it won't be a habit with you; after all, you're not like those hard-core AA folks. And besides, alcohol is not your problem—it's your husband or your kids or your lack of family or your job or money or this crazy, chaotic world we live in. Deep down you feel insecure, lonely, or out of control with your life. Those are your bigger issues, and alcohol is just a hobby that smoothes out those stressors.

Or maybe you are in a car accident and injure your back, so the doctor prescribes pain meds. You start taking them, and meanwhile, you are trying everything else you can think of to make the pain go away—chiropractors and exercise and acupuncture—but nothing is helping, and your pain is so bad you can barely function. You take more of those painkillers at each dose, and you start dosing more frequently, and before you know it, you are addicted. You're seeing multiple doctors just to get enough. You are telling yourself, "I'm in pain. I need these." You are sure that just as soon as some doctor somewhere fixes your back, you'll be done with them.

Addictions of all kinds are gripping women everywhere, and Christian women are not immune. They don't set out to become addicted, and most would never in a million years believe it could happen to them. They're not consciously looking to escape—but when they stumble upon a formula that works to dull their senses, numb their pain, and prevent them from thinking, feeling, and experiencing life, they keep coming back for more. The addictive substance soon takes over, making it no longer an issue of choice or control.

## KEEPING THE SECRET

If you are addicted to a substance, you are most likely feeling a great sense of shame. If anyone knew, they probably wouldn't believe it. It would destroy their image of you, kill their faith in you. Nobody would respect you. You fear you would lose your job or your position in the church.

We all have the image of the alcoholic—someone who is bedraggled and unkempt, unable to brush her hair or put on decent clothes. You are far from that! And so are most women who struggle with alcohol or drug addiction. Like the Meg Ryan character, you show up at school and church functions on time and put together. You perform at your job just fine, thank you very much (most of the time, anyway), and you certainly are not lying in a gutter somewhere.

Your life depends on keeping your secret. Your *secret* depends on keeping your secret. The last thing you want is for anybody to find out because then you'd have to admit it, and then maybe you'd even have to give it up . . . your vice, your crutch, your beloved wine or Vicodin or apple martini. Even the thought of giving it up brings you anxiety. Rehab? Isn't that for *real* addicts? It's certainly not for you.

You probably have moments of blinding awareness of your predicament, like when you wake in a hungover fog, unmotivated to start another day and wondering what time you're going to be able to sneak your first drink. But your denial muscle has been working overtime, and it's very strong. You're fine, really. You can quit when-ever you want. You just don't want to. But continuing down this path requires you keep it hidden. Nobody can find out! How long are you going to be able to keep up this charade?

## Think About It

Are you keeping the secret of a substance addiction? If so, I imagine that keeping this hidden is using up vast amounts of energy and emotional resources. Wouldn't it be a relief to just stop fighting? Stop trying to hold it all together for once?

Unless you've been living under a rock, you're well aware of the destructive nature of alcoholism. You know all about twelve-step and other programs that exist to help. Yet you can't bring yourself to go there—both because you don't want to give up your secret and destroy people's image of you and because you don't want to give up your drug.

But giving up your secret is the only way to healing.

> I am a sixty-one-years-young Christian woman who is a
> grateful recovering alcoholic. Through the grace of God
> and the fellowship of AA, I have been sober for almost two
> years now.

There is help for you, but you have to want it. You have to realize that this addiction and all the side effects, as bad as they are, are not the problem but symptoms of your deeper issues. You've used your addiction as a way of coping with the pain, anger, frustration, shame, and/or helplessness in your life, and now, despite your initial prob-lems, your addiction has taken on a life of its own. Life got to be too much—as it does for most of us at some time or another—and you needed to get away.

But the world needs you back.

And God wants you back.

God wants you to worship *Him* again. With addiction, you have made something else—the alcohol or the drug—your god. You've made something besides God, something besides love, central in your life. Easy to do. Harder to undo.

Edward T. Welch, Christian psychologist and author of *Addictions: A Banquet in the Grave*, views addiction as a worship disorder. Will you worship your own desires, or the one true God? Worshiping anything or anyone besides God means you have an idol, and idol worship is slavery. You are not free; you're entrapped.[1] The apostle Paul wrote, "It is for freedom that Christ has set us free. Stand firm, then, and do not let yourselves be burdened again by a yoke of slavery" (Gal. 5:1). Do you want to be free from this slavery?

Freedom will come through humbling yourself, admitting your vulnerability, and facing your powerlessness. This is one of the hardest things to do, since you went into your addiction trying to deal with some type of vulnerability. You wanted to avoid it. You wanted power and control over your life, but the answer is now the opposite: admitting you have no power over this. Admit you need to let go of this secret, let God in, and let others in.

It can be really overwhelming to get proper help, but it's virtually impossible to break a chemical addiction by yourself. You cannot get out of it by prayer alone. You cannot get out of it by willpower alone or discipline or by trying harder. You need community because it's going to get hard before it gets easier, and you need the support and encouragement of others.

Your healing will come when you choose to let go of your secret, and that will happen when you decide to accept responsibility for where you are, and where you want to go. You're going to need to admit that you are the problem, and God is the answer.

## SPIRITUAL SECRETS

Philip Yancey, in his book *Soul Survivor*, includes a profile of writer and philosopher G. K. Chesterton, who was asked to submit an essay answering the question, "What's wrong with the world?" Chesterton's contribution took the form of a letter:

> Dear Sirs,
> I am.
> Sincerely yours,
> G. K. Chesterton[2]

When you can honestly say, "I am the problem," overcoming the denials and excuses and rationalizations, you will be well on your way to healing.

Jesus asked the invalid, "Do you want to get well?" (John 5:6). He asks the same of you today. Look at your life. Think about it. As Dr. Phil would say, "How's that working for you?" Is your way of coping working? Is it providing you with a life of joy and peace?

There is hope for a new beginning. The solution is found in community, and in Jesus.

> My secret is regarding my disease of alcoholism and the fear of sharing this "new identity" with my friends at church. We recently installed a new pastor, and just yesterday I was given the opportunity to share my story with him—what an awesome blessing God gave me to have this weight lifted right off my shoulders! Now I have to face my fears to let others know how our good and gracious Lord has healed me. I know He will provide me with the opportunity and the words to do this. Healing and growing is an ongoing process, and I know that I am right where I should be according to His plan. All glory to our Lord!

## From Secrets to Solutions

At the beginning of this chapter, there is a quote from a woman who wrote to the Secrets Blog. She was addicted to alcohol but feared coming clean in her church because of the possible rejection and isolation that might result. This woman is in enough pain, I'm sure she can hardly contemplate the loss of the spiritual community in which she is comfortable and accepted. It's awful to think that this could happen, but our churches are made of imperfect people who haven't learned the meaning of love and prefer to judge others.

As difficult as it would be to face that judgment, you have to ask yourself, What is your life worth? It would be painful to lose the friends in the church, but then again, if they are going to be unloving and unsupportive, you aren't losing much. However, there's always the chance they might surprise you. You might get support and love you never knew existed. People who go through a devastating "fall from grace" usually experience the unexpected blessing of finding out who their true friends really are. Please don't let the fears stop you from going from secrets to solutions.

*Be honest with yourself.* Admit you have a problem and you need help. You don't have to go any further than that on your own—you'll get help for the next steps. Just own it: "I have a problem, and I can't deal with it on my own."

*Be honest with God.* If prayer is hard right now, just use the same statement ("I have a problem . . .") and address it to God. If you can go further than that, confess your struggle to Him, even if you aren't ready to call it an addiction, tell Him you desperately want to be healed, and ask Him to lead you to healing.

*Be honest with someone else.* Who will be supportive? Start by just telling one person. Pick your safest friend or someone who has sensitivity for others. Chances are she might already have suspected your addiction (we don't always hide things as well as we think). Make a pact with yourself and your friend to be accountable and to take the steps to break out of your isolation. Visit an open AA meeting, with or without your friend, just for educational purposes. You can just observe; you don't have to say or admit a thing. Examine your heart and ask God to nudge you if anything said fits for you. Look at local church resources for recovery groups, or go online and find an AA meeting near you. Many are held in churches but are independent of that church. Visit one at a different church so you can feel anonymous. Start small, but start to do something. Seek out others who are farther along and can help you find the right support group or AA meeting. Pick up the phone. Make the call.

## Praying Scripture for Your Secret

Pray Proverbs 28:13 and Lamentations 3:22–23.

> Lord, You have said that the one who conceals his sins does not prosper, but whoever confesses and renounces them finds mercy. I confess the sin of my addiction, Lord, and I renounce it. Your Word also says that Your compassions never fail; they are new every morning. I need Your compassion and mercy. Fill me, Lord, every morning from now on with Your compassion as I embark on this journey. Amen.

## Recommended Resources

### Support Groups
Alcoholics Anonymous—www.alcoholics-anonymous.org
    For local phone number, see your phone book
There are twelve-step groups specifically for many different drug
    addictions: Narcotics Anonymous, Cocaine Anonymous,
    Marijuana Anonymous, and so on. These are easily found
    through Internet searches and by checking your phone book

### Books
*Addictions: A Banquet in the Grave: Finding Hope in the Power of the Gospel* by Edward T. Welch
*Feeding Your Appetites: Satisfy Your Wants, Needs, and Desires Without Compromising Yourself* by Stephen Arterburn, Debbie Cherry

*Freedom from Addiction: Breaking the Bondage of Addiction and More Finding Freedom in Christ* by Neil T. Anderson, Mike Quarles, Julia Quarles, Terry Whalin

*Life's Healing Choices* by John Baker

*The Healing Path: How the Hurts in Your Past Can Lead You to a More Abundant Life* by Dan B. Allender

*The Last Addiction: Own Your Desire, Live Beyond Recovery, Find Lasting Freedom* by Sharon Hersh

*The Life Recovery Bible* edited by Steve Arterburn and Dave Stoop

*The Life Recovery Workbook: A Biblical Guide Through the Twelve Steps* by Stephen Arterburn, David Stoop

*The Twelve-Step Life Recovery Devotional* by David A. Stoop, Stephen Arterburn

# Conclusion

# Out of the Dark, Into the Light

The funny thing about writing this book is that I realized early on I would not be able to write it from a distant perspective. The responses to the Secrets Blog were heart wrenching, and I often felt convicted to pray as I read and reread them. Women are suffering with their hidden burdens, and my heart aches for their secrets to be released and for women to move toward fuller, more authentic lives. Thinking back over years of clinical experience with clients also affected me, as I was both sad for all the pain and thankful that I'd seen countless women do the hard work of letting their secrets go and finding freedom and new life on the other side.

But it wasn't just the experiences of other women that made this book a sometimes-harrowing experience. I found that there is something in almost all the secrets that I could understand and relate to, perhaps not that I share the exact secret but that each one touched something in me, struck a chord of understanding. We all want so desperately to keep our less-than-perfect selves hidden, and yet we long to be fully known. We crave deep understanding from another human, and we want to be loved despite our flaws. That's the underlying theme of this book—the need to be loved and accepted. The need to take the risk and reveal who we really are, and see that we are still lovable.

I don't know why we always think we're alone in our pain, or that nobody else could understand our experience, but somehow we do. Pain and shame are isolating; they make us instinctively want to hide ourselves. But the more we can be real and let people in, the more we realize that others are a mess too. We can stop taking ourselves so seriously. We can let a little more out. When we reveal a secret, others often reflect back on their own experiences. They say, "Yeah, me too!" and not only is a connection formed, but people feel more real and authentic, validated, and less alone.

I wrote about numerous types of secrets in this book, and one thing I wanted to mention is how so many of them are tied together. Most people carry secrets in several categories, and this is because the secrets overlap and are related to one another. Wounds from our past cause us to suffer or act out in our adult life, sometimes in multiple ways. Eating disorders are often tied with sexual abuse as a child. Current relationship problems may be related to past sexual promiscuity. Financial problems burden almost everyone, and are sometimes related to other secrets, such as feeling invisible or discontented with life. There's a good chance that you can relate to ten of the fifteen categories of secrets represented here, and if so, don't feel that that makes you odd.

There are also several categories of secrets I wasn't able to address in the book because of space limitations. If you are burdened by something I didn't address, I hope you understand that the principles are the same regardless of the secret with which you're dealing. Keeping the secret is eroding your happiness and emotional health. Only by opening the secret box and sharing it appropriately—with self, God, and someone else—can you hope to live a life of joy and integrity, a life in which you are the same on the outside as on the inside.

Your secret doesn't define you. It's not *who you are*. Your identity is in Christ, and "there is now no condemnation for those who are in Christ Jesus" (Rom. 8:1). So I want to finish by exhorting you, above all, to keep your eyes on Jesus.

Get connected spiritually by reading Scripture, praying, and creating space to hear God speaking.

Get connected emotionally by seeking support from others. Face the fear of being vulnerable. Take the risk of opening up. Seek wise counsel if you need it, from a pastor, counselor, or friend. We're not meant to deal with problems in our lives alone. We're meant to do it with one another. It's why Christ came, to show us the way. He came to be with us, so that we wouldn't have to find the way all by ourselves. So make sure you are connecting emotionally.

Stay connected with yourself. Keep working to be honest with yourself. Confront your denials and resistances, and try to uncover the secrets you keep from yourself.

And now, "May the God of hope fill you with all joy and peace as you trust in him, so that you may overflow with hope by the power of the Holy Spirit" (Rom. 15:13). Joy, peace, and hope. That is my prayer for you.

*Afterword*

———

# by Steve Arterburn

I know this book has been an intense journey. I hope you've found comfort in knowing that whatever your secret, thousands of women share it. You are not alone, and healing comes through letting the secrets go, opening up, and letting in others who can help you.

If you've read through this book quickly and skimmed over the suggestions at the end of each chapter, I encourage you to stop now and make a plan. What are you going to do—specifically—to begin unburdening yourself of your secrets? You are a unique individual, so your plan may not look like anyone else's. This is all yours.

You may want to start by journaling or simply making a list of the things you keep as "secrets," those little pieces of truth about yourself or your life that you carry privately and they weigh on you. What are they? Grab a notebook or open a fresh page on your computer and start writing.

Think about the ways you might begin to share yourself more fully with others. Do you need to connect with other women more regularly or more deeply? Would it help to seek counseling? The Bible has a lot to say about living a life free from hiding. Maybe you'll want to begin an investigation into what God's Word says.

Dr. Jill has made clear throughout this book that becoming free of secrets doesn't mean you "let it all hang out." It doesn't mean you have to tell everybody everything about you. But it does mean you have a safe place in which to be fully *you*. If you don't have this, life will be unbearably lonely because it means there's no true relational connecting going on.

Secrets have a way of catching up with us. There's an old saying, "The truth will come out," and it's true—we are rarely able to keep a secret all the way to the grave. The Bible emphasizes that God knows everything about us, even our deepest, darkest secrets: "Nothing in all creation is hidden from God's sight. Everything is uncovered and laid bare before the eyes of him to whom we must give account" (Heb. 4:13).

The significant thing is that not only does God know all our secrets—He loves us anyway. We keep secrets because we fear the consequences of others fully knowing what's in our hearts and minds, but it's amazing to realize God *knows it all* and He completely accepts us.

May God be with you as you go forward in pursuit of a secret-free life, and may He grant you freedom, peace, and grace as you move from secrets to solutions.

To contact New Life:
1-800-New Life
www.newlife.com

# Acknowledgments

What a kick it is for me to be writing this page because in reflecting on the people I want to acknowledge in the making of this book, I realize . . . I'm almost finished!

From the moment Steve Arterburn said that he had the perfect project for me, life has been a whirlwind. Dinner was lined up with Greg Johnson of WordServe Literary, and shortly thereafter I was introduced to Thomas Nelson, Inc. through the kind gentleman of Joey Paul. Thanks to each of them for knowing that this book was in my future and for opening the doors I needed to walk through. Especially to Steve for all his prodding and poking, for respecting no limits on the tactics he would try, for convincing me to take the leap into the writing world . . . *thank you.*

My heartfelt gratitude to the radio audience of *New Life Live!* and to the women who responded so willingly to our Secrets Blog: you were the catalyst to the research for this book; you confirmed the felt need and contributed greatly by speaking openly from your hearts.

To the New Life staff and volunteers, both past and present, who serve faithfully for the good of the ministry, who are always eager to help as needed—from resource ideas to technical support to brainstorming to telling me where to be and at what time. I so appreciate you in the behind-the-scenes roles you play.

To my clients through the years who have taught me so much through your experiences and given me a greater capacity for compassion, thank you for all that I have gleaned from your honest vulnerability in sharing your secrets with me.

Writing something of meaning draws forth a culmination of experience that is tightly wrapped around the writer's main artery. I believe in practicing what I preach and could not ask readers to risk their secrets if I dared not share my own, and in so doing, I know the pain that secrets can cause. Therefore, I sincerely thank the secret bearers who have walked with me. To my mentors, Nancy Anne Smith, PsyD, who has given a lifetime of wisdom and taught me through her unwavering constancy; and to Christal Daehnert, PhD, PsyD, who in her calming way has taught me how to listen insightfully and reflect back a voice of compassion. To a fellow counselor, Ryan Patrick Murphy, Esq, who helps good people—in the worst times of their lives—pick up the pieces after the exploding of their secrets. To Mike Marino, PhD, for his communication skills, expertise, and enduring friendship. To my supportive family members, who are always willing to throw in their two cents. And special thanks to my kids, Noelle and Mack, who—at eleven and six years of age—endured "boring days, cuz Mom was working on her book again!" I thank my dear friends, who live life with me and for the mutual camaraderie of bearing one another's secrets, especially the four Damas, who at times have been my own lifeline.

This endeavor, as most things we labor over, has taught me much. It has been a navigation of my own strengths and weaknesses. I have learned that the writing and producing of a book, though it may not take a village, certainly takes a team. My team is worth its weight in gold. Each team member set me up to capitalize on what I do best and helped fill in the gaps where I floundered. Special thanks to my spirited editor, Debbie Wickwire, for giving me a crash course in publishing 101 and for loving this project. And my sincerest gratitude to the many other people at Thomas Nelson whose hands this project has passed through. It truly has been a collaborative process!

My biggest thanks go to Rachelle Gardner, who partnered with me and guided each step and without whom the words on the page would not have formed a book. From the formulating and categorizing of our research to the hours we spent dialoging about what women struggle with most, she put her heart into this work. She agonized over and felt the pain of the women's stories that touched a chord in both of us, causing reflection of our own. Thanks to her husband and daughters who surely felt the burden and picked up the slack for her under the demand of deadlines. Thanks, Rachelle, for your continued graciousness with me as I worked at my own unique pace. You are a genuine person of depth and a writer extraordinaire.

# Notes

CHAPTER 1: EVERYONE HAS SECRETS
1. Tammy Maltby, *Confessions of a Good Christian Girl* (Nashville: Thomas Nelson, 2007), 7.
2. Gail Saltz, MD, *Anatomy of a Secret Life* (New York: Morgan Road, 2006), 43.

CHAPTER 3: KEEPING SECRETS FROM OURSELVES
1. Henry Cloud, *Changes that Heal* (Grand Rapids: Zondervan, 1997).

CHAPTER 4: I'M UNHAPPY IN MY MARRIAGE
1. Gary Thomas, *Sacred Marriage* (Grand Rapids: Zondervan, 2000), 13.

CHAPTER 5: I'VE HAD AN EMOTIONAL OR PHYSICAL AFFAIR
1. Gail Saltz, MD, *Anatomy of a Secret Life* (New York: Morgan Road, 2006), 59.
2. Janis A. Spring, *After the Affair* (New York: Harper Collins, 1996), 6.
3. Beryl Singleton Bissell, *The Scent of God* (New York: Perseus, 2006), 89.
4. Sharon Souza, *Every Good and Perfect Gift* (Colorado Springs: NavPress, 2007), 172.
5. Milan and Kay Yerkovich, *How We Love* (Colorado Springs: Waterbrook, 2006), 239.

CHAPTER 6: MY PARTNER USES PORNOGRAPHY OR HAS HAD AN AFFAIR
1. Tammy Maltby, *Confessions of a Good Christian Girl* (Nashville: Thomas Nelson, 2007), 67.
2. Clay and Renee Cross, *I Surrender All* (Colorado Springs: NavPress, 2005), 74.
3. Fred and Brenda Stoeker with Mike Yorkey, *Every Heart Restored* (Colorado Springs: WaterBrook, 2004), 21.
4. Dr. Henry Cloud and Dr. Henry Townsend, *Boundaries in Marriage* (Grand Rapids: Zondervan, 2002), 134.
5. Ibid., 254.
6. Fred and Brenda Stoeker, *Every Heart Restored*, 35.

CHAPTER 7: BEING SINGLE WAS NOT MY DREAM
1. Audrey Barrick, "Single Women Outnumber Married; Happier Single?" *Christian Post Reporter,* January 19, 2007; available at www.christianpost.com/article/20070119/25283_Single_Women_Outnumber_Married%3B_Happier_Single%3F.htm. "The Census Bureau's latest American Community Survey revealed that among the more than 117 million women over the age of

15, 63 million are married. Of those, 3.1 million are legally separated and 2.4 million said their husbands were not living at home for one reason or another. This leaves the number of women living with a spouse at 57.5 million."

2. Gary Chapman, *Five Love Languages for Singles* (Chicago: Moody, 2004), 12.
3. Philip Yancey, *Where Is God When It Hurts?* (Grand Rapids: Zondervan, 2002), 200.
4. Michelle McKinney Hammond, *How to Avoid the 10 Mistakes Single Women Make* (Eugene, OR: Harvest House, 2006), multiple pages.

CHAPTER 8: FRIENDSHIP ISN'T EASY

1. Marion K. Underwood, *Social Aggression Among Girls* (New York: Guilford Press, 2003), 4–6.
2. Jeff Wickwire, *Friendships: Avoiding the Ones that Hurt, Finding the Ones that Heal* (Grand Rapids: Baker, 2007), 16.
3. C. S. Lewis, *The Four Loves,* Harcourt Brace Modern Classics Edition (Orlando: Harcourt, 1960, 1988), 62.
4. Tracy Klehn, *Growing Friendships: Connecting More Deeply with Those Who Matter Most* (Minneapolis: Bethany House, 2007), 19; emphasis in original.

CHAPTER 9: MY HUSBAND AND I HAVE DIFFERENT SEXUAL NEEDS

1. Excerpt from *The Sex-Starved Wife* by Michele Weiner Davis (New York: Simon & Schuster, 2006), msnbc.com, www.msnbc.msn.com/id/22492002/page/2; accessed 3/1/08.
2. Ibid.
3. Dr. Linda Mintle, *Divorce-Proofing Your Marriage: 10 Lies that Will Lead to Divorce and 10 Truths that Will Stop It* (Lake Mary, FL: Strang, 2001).
4. Gary Chapman, *The Five Love Languages* (Chicago: Moody, 2004), 115.

CHAPTER 10: I STRUGGLE WITH SEXUAL ADDICTION

1. John W. Kennedy, "Help for the Sexually Desperate," *Christianity Today* 52, no. 3 (March 2008): 28; available at www.christianitytoday.com/ct/2008/march/18.28.html.
2. Daniel Amen, *Sex on the Brain: 12 Lessons to Enhance Your Love Life* (New York: Harmony, 2007).
3. Kennedy, "Help for the Sexually Desperate," *Christianity Today.*

CHAPTER 11: I'M DISCONTENTED WITH LIFE

1. *Matthew Henry's Commentary on the Whole Bible* (McLean, VA: Mac Donald, n.d.), 694.
2. J. P. Moreland and Klaus Issler, *The Lost Virtue of Happiness* (Colorado Springs: NavPress, 2006), 25.

3. Jennifer Hecht, *The Happiness Myth* (New York: Harper Collins, 2007), 3–4.
4. M. Scott Peck, *The Road Less Traveled* (New York: Simon & Schuster, 1978), 15.
5. Rob Bell, *Sex God* (Grand Rapids.: Zondervan, 2007), 46.

CHAPTER 12: I STRUGGLE WITH SPIRITUAL DISCONNECT
1. Patricia Raybon, *I Told the Mountain to Move* (Carol Stream, IL: Tyndale, 2006), 173.

CHAPTER 15: I OBSESS OVER MY WEIGHT AND EATING
1. Stephen Arterburn and Dr. Linda Mintle, *Lose It for Life* (Nashville: Integrity, 2004), xiv.
2. Claire Cloninger and Laura Barr, *Faithfully Fit* (Dallas: Word, 1991), 12.
3. Ibid., 15.

CHAPTER 16: MY PAST HAUNTS ME
1. Dan Allender, *The Wounded Heart* (Colorado Springs: NavPress, 1995), 43.
2. "Abortion in the United States: Statistics and Trends," National Right to Life; statistics based on CDC and AGI figures, 1973–present; available at www.nrlc.org/abortion/facts/abortionstats.html.
3. David A. Stoop, *Forgiving the Unforgivable* (Ventura, CA: Regal, 2005), 16.
4. C. S. Lewis, letter to Miss Breckenridge, 19 April 1951, *The Collected Letters of C. S. Lewis, Volume III: Narnia, Cambridge, and Joy 1950–1963*, Walter Hooper (ed.) (San Francisco: HarperOne, 2007), 109.
5. Dan Allender, *The Wounded Heart* (Colorado Springs: NavPress, 1995), 45.

CHAPTER 17: I WORRY ABOUT FINANCES
1. Suze Orman, *The 9 Steps to Financial Freedom: Practical and Spiritual Steps So You Can Stop Worrying* (New York: Crown, 1997), 3.
2. Larry Burkett, *Money Matters* (Nashville: Thomas Nelson, 2001), 3.
3. © Olivia Mellan, 2007, "Money and Gender—Therapists and Clients," Zur Institute, www.zurinstitute.com/online/fees5.html; accessed April 28, 2008.
4. First Timothy 6:10 says, "For the *love of money* is a root of all kinds of evil" (emphasis added)—not money itself but the love of it.
5. "What does the Bible say about managing your finances?" GotQuestions.org, www.gotquestions.org/managing-finances.html.
6. Orman, *The 9 Steps to Financial Freedom*, 35.
7. Burkett, *Money Matters*, 228.

CHAPTER 18: I STRUGGLE WITH ALCOHOL OR DRUG ADDICTION
1. Edward T. Welch, *Addictions: A Banquet in the Grave* (Phillipsburg, NJ: P&R, 2001).
2. Philip Yancey, *Soul Survivor* (New York: Doubleday, 2003), 58.